Mometrix
TEST PREPARATION

I0891979

Series 99

Exam Secrets Study Guide

DEAR FUTURE EXAM SUCCESS STORY

First of all, **THANK YOU** for purchasing Mometrix study materials!

Second, congratulations! You are one of the few determined test-takers who are committed to doing whatever it takes to excel on your exam. **You have come to the right place.** We developed these study materials with one goal in mind: to deliver you the information you need in a format that's concise and easy to use.

In addition to optimizing your guide for the content of the test, we've outlined our recommended steps for breaking down the preparation process into small, attainable goals so you can make sure you stay on track.

We've also analyzed the entire test-taking process, identifying the most common pitfalls and showing how you can overcome them and be ready for any curveball the test throws you.

Standardized testing is one of the biggest obstacles on your road to success, which only increases the importance of doing well in the high-pressure, high-stakes environment of test day. Your results on this test could have a significant impact on your future, and this guide provides the information and practical advice to help you achieve your full potential on test day.

Your success is our success

We would love to hear from you! If you would like to share the story of your exam success or if you have any questions or comments in regard to our products, please contact us at **800-673-8175** or **support@mometrix.com**.

Thanks again for your business and we wish you continued success!

Sincerely,
The Mometrix Test Preparation Team

Need more help? Check out our flashcards at:
http://MometrixFlashcards.com/Series99

Written and edited by the Mometrix Exam Secrets Test Prep Team
Printed in the United States of America

TABLE OF CONTENTS

Introduction

Thank you for purchasing this resource! You have made the choice to prepare yourself for a test that could have a huge impact on your future, and this guide is designed to help you be fully ready for test day. Obviously, it's important to have a solid understanding of the test material, but you also need to be prepared for the unique environment and stressors of the test, so that you can perform to the best of your abilities.

For this purpose, the first section that appears in this guide is the **Secret Keys**. We've devoted countless hours to meticulously researching what works and what doesn't, and we've boiled down our findings to the five most impactful steps you can take to improve your performance on the test. We start at the beginning with study planning and move through the preparation process, all the way to the testing strategies that will help you get the most out of what you know when you're finally sitting in front of the test.

We recommend that you start preparing for your test as far in advance as possible. However, if you've bought this guide as a last-minute study resource and only have a few days before your test, we recommend that you skip over the first two Secret Keys since they address a long-term study plan.

If you struggle with **test anxiety**, we strongly encourage you to check out our recommendations for how you can overcome it. Test anxiety is a formidable foe, but it can be beaten, and we want to make sure you have the tools you need to defeat it.

Secret Key 1: Plan Big, Study Small

There's a lot riding on your performance. If you want to ace this test, you're going to need to keep your skills sharp and the material fresh in your mind. You need a plan that lets you review everything you need to know while still fitting in your schedule. We'll break this strategy down into three categories.

Information Organization

Start with the information you already have: the official test outline. From this, you can make a complete list of all the concepts you need to cover before the test. Organize these concepts into groups that can be studied together, and create a list of any related vocabulary you need to learn so you can brush up on any difficult terms. You'll want to keep this vocabulary list handy once you actually start studying since you may need to add to it along the way.

Time Management

Once you have your set of study concepts, decide how to spread them out over the time you have left before the test. Break your study plan into small, clear goals so you have a manageable task for each day and know exactly what you're doing. Then just focus on one small step at a time. When you manage your time this way, you don't need to spend hours at a time studying. Studying a small block of content for a short period each day helps you retain information better and avoid stressing over how much you have left to do. You can relax knowing that you have a plan to cover everything in time. In order for this strategy to be effective though, you have to start studying early and stick to your schedule. Avoid the exhaustion and futility that comes from last-minute cramming!

Study Environment

The environment you study in has a big impact on your learning. Studying in a coffee shop, while probably more enjoyable, is not likely to be as fruitful as studying in a quiet room. It's important to keep distractions to a minimum. You're only planning to study for a short block of time, so make the most of it. Don't pause to check your phone or get up to find a snack. It's also important to **avoid multitasking**. Research has consistently shown that multitasking will make your studying dramatically less effective. Your study area should also be comfortable and well-lit so you don't have the distraction of straining your eyes or sitting on an uncomfortable chair.

The time of day you study is also important. You want to be rested and alert. Don't wait until just before bedtime. Study when you'll be most likely to comprehend and remember. Even better, if you know what time of day your test will be, set that time aside for study. That way your brain will be used to working on that subject at that specific time and you'll have a better chance of recalling information.

Finally, it can be helpful to team up with others who are studying for the same test. Your actual studying should be done in as isolated an environment as possible, but the work of organizing the information and setting up the study plan can be divided up. In between study sessions, you can discuss with your teammates the concepts that you're all studying and quiz each other on the details. Just be sure that your teammates are as serious about the test as you are. If you find that your study time is being replaced with social time, you might need to find a new team.

Secret Key 2: Make Your Studying Count

You're devoting a lot of time and effort to preparing for this test, so you want to be absolutely certain it will pay off. This means doing more than just reading the content and hoping you can remember it on test day. It's important to make every minute of study count. There are two main areas you can focus on to make your studying count.

Retention

It doesn't matter how much time you study if you can't remember the material. You need to make sure you are retaining the concepts. To check your retention of the information you're learning, try recalling it at later times with minimal prompting. Try carrying around flashcards and glance at one or two from time to time or ask a friend who's also studying for the test to quiz you.

To enhance your retention, look for ways to put the information into practice so that you can apply it rather than simply recalling it. If you're using the information in practical ways, it will be much easier to remember. Similarly, it helps to solidify a concept in your mind if you're not only reading it to yourself but also explaining it to someone else. Ask a friend to let you teach them about a concept you're a little shaky on (or speak aloud to an imaginary audience if necessary). As you try to summarize, define, give examples, and answer your friend's questions, you'll understand the concepts better and they will stay with you longer. Finally, step back for a big picture view and ask yourself how each piece of information fits with the whole subject. When you link the different concepts together and see them working together as a whole, it's easier to remember the individual components.

Finally, practice showing your work on any multi-step problems, even if you're just studying. Writing out each step you take to solve a problem will help solidify the process in your mind, and you'll be more likely to remember it during the test.

Modality

Modality simply refers to the means or method by which you study. Choosing a study modality that fits your own individual learning style is crucial. No two people learn best in exactly the same way, so it's important to know your strengths and use them to your advantage.

For example, if you learn best by visualization, focus on visualizing a concept in your mind and draw an image or a diagram. Try color-coding your notes, illustrating them, or creating symbols that will trigger your mind to recall a learned concept. If you learn best by hearing or discussing information, find a study partner who learns the same way or read aloud to yourself. Think about how to put the information in your own words. Imagine that you are giving a lecture on the topic and record yourself so you can listen to it later.

For any learning style, flashcards can be helpful. Organize the information so you can take advantage of spare moments to review. Underline key words or phrases. Use different colors for different categories. Mnemonic devices (such as creating a short list in which every item starts with the same letter) can also help with retention. Find what works best for you and use it to store the information in your mind most effectively and easily.

Secret Key 3: Practice the Right Way

Your success on test day depends not only on how many hours you put into preparing, but also on whether you prepared the right way. It's good to check along the way to see if your studying is paying off. One of the most effective ways to do this is by taking practice tests to evaluate your progress. Practice tests are useful because they show exactly where you need to improve. Every time you take a practice test, pay special attention to these three groups of questions:

- The questions you got wrong
- The questions you had to guess on, even if you guessed right
- The questions you found difficult or slow to work through

This will show you exactly what your weak areas are, and where you need to devote more study time. Ask yourself why each of these questions gave you trouble. Was it because you didn't understand the material? Was it because you didn't remember the vocabulary? Do you need more repetitions on this type of question to build speed and confidence? Dig into those questions and figure out how you can strengthen your weak areas as you go back to review the material.

Additionally, many practice tests have a section explaining the answer choices. It can be tempting to read the explanation and think that you now have a good understanding of the concept. However, an explanation likely only covers part of the question's broader context. Even if the explanation makes perfect sense, **go back and investigate** every concept related to the question until you're positive you have a thorough understanding.

As you go along, keep in mind that the practice test is just that: practice. Memorizing these questions and answers will not be very helpful on the actual test because it is unlikely to have any of the same exact questions. If you only know the right answers to the sample questions, you won't be prepared for the real thing. **Study the concepts** until you understand them fully, and then you'll be able to answer any question that shows up on the test.

It's important to wait on the practice tests until you're ready. If you take a test on your first day of study, you may be overwhelmed by the amount of material covered and how much you need to learn. Work up to it gradually.

On test day, you'll need to be prepared for answering questions, managing your time, and using the test-taking strategies you've learned. It's a lot to balance, like a mental marathon that will have a big impact on your future. Like training for a marathon, you'll need to start slowly and work your way up. When test day arrives, you'll be ready.

Start with the strategies you've read in the first two Secret Keys—plan your course and study in the way that works best for you. If you have time, consider using multiple study resources to get different approaches to the same concepts. It can be helpful to see difficult concepts from more than one angle. Then find a good source for practice tests. Many times, the test website will suggest potential study resources or provide sample tests.

Practice Test Strategy

If you're able to find at least three practice tests, we recommend this strategy:

UNTIMED AND OPEN-BOOK PRACTICE

Take the first test with no time constraints and with your notes and study guide handy. Take your time and focus on applying the strategies you've learned.

TIMED AND OPEN-BOOK PRACTICE

Take the second practice test open-book as well, but set a timer and practice pacing yourself to finish in time.

TIMED AND CLOSED-BOOK PRACTICE

Take any other practice tests as if it were test day. Set a timer and put away your study materials. Sit at a table or desk in a quiet room, imagine yourself at the testing center, and answer questions as quickly and accurately as possible.

Keep repeating timed and closed-book tests on a regular basis until you run out of practice tests or it's time for the actual test. Your mind will be ready for the schedule and stress of test day, and you'll be able to focus on recalling the material you've learned.

Secret Key 4: Pace Yourself

Once you're fully prepared for the material on the test, your biggest challenge on test day will be managing your time. Just knowing that the clock is ticking can make you panic even if you have plenty of time left. Work on pacing yourself so you can build confidence against the time constraints of the exam. Pacing is a difficult skill to master, especially in a high-pressure environment, so **practice is vital**.

Set time expectations for your pace based on how much time is available. For example, if a section has 60 questions and the time limit is 30 minutes, you know you have to average 30 seconds or less per question in order to answer them all. Although 30 seconds is the hard limit, set 25 seconds per question as your goal, so you reserve extra time to spend on harder questions. When you budget extra time for the harder questions, you no longer have any reason to stress when those questions take longer to answer.

Don't let this time expectation distract you from working through the test at a calm, steady pace, but keep it in mind so you don't spend too much time on any one question. Recognize that taking extra time on one question you don't understand may keep you from answering two that you do understand later in the test. If your time limit for a question is up and you're still not sure of the answer, mark it and move on, and come back to it later if the time and the test format allow. If the testing format doesn't allow you to return to earlier questions, just make an educated guess; then put it out of your mind and move on.

On the easier questions, be careful not to rush. It may seem wise to hurry through them so you have more time for the challenging ones, but it's not worth missing one if you know the concept and just didn't take the time to read the question fully. Work efficiently but make sure you understand the question and have looked at all of the answer choices, since more than one may seem right at first.

Even if you're paying attention to the time, you may find yourself a little behind at some point. You should speed up to get back on track, but do so wisely. Don't panic; just take a few seconds less on each question until you're caught up. Don't guess without thinking, but do look through the answer choices and eliminate any you know are wrong. If you can get down to two choices, it is often worthwhile to guess from those. Once you've chosen an answer, move on and don't dwell on any that you skipped or had to hurry through. If a question was taking too long, chances are it was one of the harder ones, so you weren't as likely to get it right anyway.

On the other hand, if you find yourself getting ahead of schedule, it may be beneficial to slow down a little. The more quickly you work, the more likely you are to make a careless mistake that will affect your score. You've budgeted time for each question, so don't be afraid to spend that time. Practice an efficient but careful pace to get the most out of the time you have.

Secret Key 5: Have a Plan for Guessing

When you're taking the test, you may find yourself stuck on a question. Some of the answer choices seem better than others, but you don't see the one answer choice that is obviously correct. What do you do?

The scenario described above is very common, yet most test takers have not effectively prepared for it. Developing and practicing a plan for guessing may be one of the single most effective uses of your time as you get ready for the exam.

In developing your plan for guessing, there are three questions to address:

- When should you start the guessing process?
- How should you narrow down the choices?
- Which answer should you choose?

When to Start the Guessing Process

Unless your plan for guessing is to select C every time (which, despite its merits, is not what we recommend), you need to leave yourself enough time to apply your answer elimination strategies. Since you have a limited amount of time for each question, that means that if you're going to give yourself the best shot at guessing correctly, you have to decide quickly whether or not you will guess.

Of course, the best-case scenario is that you don't have to guess at all, so first, see if you can answer the question based on your knowledge of the subject and basic reasoning skills. Focus on the key words in the question and try to jog your memory of related topics. Give yourself a chance to bring the knowledge to mind, but once you realize that you don't have (or you can't access) the knowledge you need to answer the question, it's time to start the guessing process.

It's almost always better to start the guessing process too early than too late. It only takes a few seconds to remember something and answer the question from knowledge. Carefully eliminating wrong answer choices takes longer. Plus, going through the process of eliminating answer choices can actually help jog your memory.

Summary: Start the guessing process as soon as you decide that you can't answer the question based on your knowledge.

How to Narrow Down the Choices

The next chapter in this book (**Test-Taking Strategies**) includes a wide range of strategies for how to approach questions and how to look for answer choices to eliminate. You will definitely want to read those carefully, practice them, and figure out which ones work best for you. Here though, we're going to address a mindset rather than a particular strategy.

Your odds of guessing an answer correctly depend on how many options you are choosing from.

Number of options left	5	4	3	2	1
Odds of guessing correctly	20%	25%	33%	50%	100%

You can see from this chart just how valuable it is to be able to eliminate incorrect answers and make an educated guess, but there are two things that many test takers do that cause them to miss out on the benefits of guessing:

- Accidentally eliminating the correct answer
- Selecting an answer based on an impression

We'll look at the first one here, and the second one in the next section.

To avoid accidentally eliminating the correct answer, we recommend a thought exercise called **the $5 challenge**. In this challenge, you only eliminate an answer choice from contention if you are willing to bet $5 on it being wrong. Why $5? Five dollars is a small but not insignificant amount of money. It's an amount you could afford to lose but wouldn't want to throw away. And while losing $5 once might not hurt too much, doing it twenty times will set you back $100. In the same way, each small decision you make—eliminating a choice here, guessing on a question there—won't by itself impact your score very much, but when you put them all together, they can make a big difference. By holding each answer choice elimination decision to a higher standard, you can reduce the risk of accidentally eliminating the correct answer.

The $5 challenge can also be applied in a positive sense: If you are willing to bet $5 that an answer choice *is* correct, go ahead and mark it as correct.

Summary: Only eliminate an answer choice if you are willing to bet $5 that it is wrong.

Which Answer to Choose

You're taking the test. You've run into a hard question and decided you'll have to guess. You've eliminated all the answer choices you're willing to bet $5 on. Now you have to pick an answer. Why do we even need to talk about this? Why can't you just pick whichever one you feel like when the time comes?

The answer to these questions is that if you don't come into the test with a plan, you'll rely on your impression to select an answer choice, and if you do that, you risk falling into a trap. The test writers know that everyone who takes their test will be guessing on some of the questions, so they intentionally write wrong answer choices to seem plausible. You still have to pick an answer though, and if the wrong answer choices are designed to look right, how can you ever be sure that you're not falling for their trap? The best solution we've found to this dilemma is to take the decision out of your hands entirely. Here is the process we recommend:

Once you've eliminated any choices that you are confident (willing to bet $5) are wrong, select the first remaining choice as your answer.

Whether you choose to select the first remaining choice, the second, or the last, the important thing is that you use some preselected standard. Using this approach guarantees that you will not be enticed into selecting an answer choice that looks right, because you are not basing your decision on how the answer choices look.

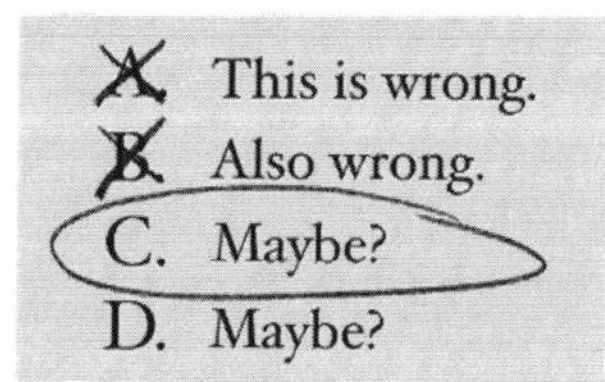

This is not meant to make you question your knowledge. Instead, it is to help you recognize the difference between your knowledge and your impressions. There's a huge difference between thinking an answer is right because of what you know, and thinking an answer is right because it looks or sounds like it should be right.

Summary: To ensure that your selection is appropriately random, make a predetermined selection from among all answer choices you have not eliminated.

Test-Taking Strategies

This section contains a list of test-taking strategies that you may find helpful as you work through the test. By taking what you know and applying logical thought, you can maximize your chances of answering any question correctly!

It is very important to realize that every question is different and every person is different: no single strategy will work on every question, and no single strategy will work for every person. That's why we've included all of them here, so you can try them out and determine which ones work best for different types of questions and which ones work best for you.

Question Strategies

✓ Read Carefully

Read the question and the answer choices carefully. Don't miss the question because you misread the terms. You have plenty of time to read each question thoroughly and make sure you understand what is being asked. Yet a happy medium must be attained, so don't waste too much time. You must read carefully and efficiently.

✓ Contextual Clues

Look for contextual clues. If the question includes a word you are not familiar with, look at the immediate context for some indication of what the word might mean. Contextual clues can often give you all the information you need to decipher the meaning of an unfamiliar word. Even if you can't determine the meaning, you may be able to narrow down the possibilities enough to make a solid guess at the answer to the question.

✓ Prefixes

If you're having trouble with a word in the question or answer choices, try dissecting it. Take advantage of every clue that the word might include. Prefixes can be a huge help. Usually, they allow you to determine a basic meaning. *Pre-* means before, *post-* means after, *pro-* is positive, *de-* is negative. From prefixes, you can get an idea of the general meaning of the word and try to put it into context.

✓ Hedge Words

Watch out for critical hedge words, such as *likely, may, can, often, almost, mostly, usually, generally, rarely,* and *sometimes.* Question writers insert these hedge phrases to cover every possibility. Often an answer choice will be wrong simply because it leaves no room for exception. Be on guard for answer choices that have definitive words such as *exactly* and *always.*

✓ Switchback Words

Stay alert for *switchbacks*. These are the words and phrases frequently used to alert you to shifts in thought. The most common switchback words are *but, although*, and *however*. Others include *nevertheless, on the other hand, even though, while, in spite of, despite*, and *regardless of*. Switchback words are important to catch because they can change the direction of the question or an answer choice.

✓ Face Value

When in doubt, use common sense. Accept the situation in the problem at face value. Don't read too much into it. These problems will not require you to make wild assumptions. If you have to go beyond creativity and warp time or space in order to have an answer choice fit the question, then you should move on and consider the other answer choices. These are normal problems rooted in reality. The applicable relationship or explanation may not be readily apparent, but it is there for you to figure out. Use your common sense to interpret anything that isn't clear.

Answer Choice Strategies

✓ Answer Selection

The most thorough way to pick an answer choice is to identify and eliminate wrong answers until only one is left, then confirm it is the correct answer. Sometimes an answer choice may immediately seem right, but be careful. The test writers will usually put more than one reasonable answer choice on each question, so take a second to read all of them and make sure that the other choices are not equally obvious. As long as you have time left, it is better to read every answer choice than to pick the first one that looks right without checking the others.

✓ Answer Choice Families

An answer choice family consists of two (in rare cases, three) answer choices that are very similar in construction and cannot all be true at the same time. If you see two answer choices that are direct opposites or parallels, one of them is usually the correct answer. For instance, if one answer choice says that quantity x increases and another either says that quantity x decreases (opposite) or says that quantity y increases (parallel), then those answer choices would fall into the same family. An answer choice that doesn't match the construction of the answer choice family is more likely to be incorrect. Most questions will not have answer choice families, but when they do appear, you should be prepared to recognize them.

✓ Eliminate Answers

Eliminate answer choices as soon as you realize they are wrong, but make sure you consider all possibilities. If you are eliminating answer choices and realize that the last one you are left with is also wrong, don't panic. Start over and consider each choice again. There may be something you missed the first time that you will realize on the second pass.

⊘ Avoid Fact Traps

Don't be distracted by an answer choice that is factually true but doesn't answer the question. You are looking for the choice that answers the question. Stay focused on what the question is asking for so you don't accidentally pick an answer that is true but incorrect. Always go back to the question and make sure the answer choice you've selected actually answers the question and is not merely a true statement.

⊘ Extreme Statements

In general, you should avoid answers that put forth extreme actions as standard practice or proclaim controversial ideas as established fact. An answer choice that states the "process should be used in certain situations, if…" is much more likely to be correct than one that states the "process should be discontinued completely." The first is a calm rational statement and doesn't even make a definitive, uncompromising stance, using a hedge word *if* to provide wiggle room, whereas the second choice is far more extreme.

⊘ Benchmark

As you read through the answer choices and you come across one that seems to answer the question well, mentally select that answer choice. This is not your final answer, but it's the one that will help you evaluate the other answer choices. The one that you selected is your benchmark or standard for judging each of the other answer choices. Every other answer choice must be compared to your benchmark. That choice is correct until proven otherwise by another answer choice beating it. If you find a better answer, then that one becomes your new benchmark. Once you've decided that no other choice answers the question as well as your benchmark, you have your final answer.

⊘ Predict the Answer

Before you even start looking at the answer choices, it is often best to try to predict the answer. When you come up with the answer on your own, it is easier to avoid distractions and traps because you will know exactly what to look for. The right answer choice is unlikely to be word-for-word what you came up with, but it should be a close match. Even if you are confident that you have the right answer, you should still take the time to read each option before moving on.

General Strategies

⊘ Tough Questions

If you are stumped on a problem or it appears too hard or too difficult, don't waste time. Move on! Remember though, if you can quickly check for obviously incorrect answer choices, your chances of guessing correctly are greatly improved. Before you completely give up, at least try to knock out a couple of possible answers. Eliminate what you can and then guess at the remaining answer choices before moving on.

⊘ Check Your Work

Since you will probably not know every term listed and the answer to every question, it is important that you get credit for the ones that you do know. Don't miss any questions through careless mistakes. If at all possible, try to take a second to look back over your answer selection and make sure you've selected the correct answer choice and haven't made a costly careless mistake (such as marking an answer choice that you didn't mean to mark). This quick double check should more than pay for itself in caught mistakes for the time it costs.

⊘ Pace Yourself

It's easy to be overwhelmed when you're looking at a page full of questions; your mind is confused and full of random thoughts, and the clock is ticking down faster than you would like. Calm down and maintain the pace that you have set for yourself. Especially as you get down to the last few minutes of the test, don't let the small numbers on the clock make you panic. As long as you are on track by monitoring your pace, you are guaranteed to have time for each question.

⊘ Don't Rush

It is very easy to make errors when you are in a hurry. Maintaining a fast pace in answering questions is pointless if it makes you miss questions that you would have gotten right otherwise. Test writers like to include distracting information and wrong answers that seem right. Taking a little extra time to avoid careless mistakes can make all the difference in your test score. Find a pace that allows you to be confident in the answers that you select.

⊘ Keep Moving

Panicking will not help you pass the test, so do your best to stay calm and keep moving. Taking deep breaths and going through the answer elimination steps you practiced can help to break through a stress barrier and keep your pace.

Final Notes

The combination of a solid foundation of content knowledge and the confidence that comes from practicing your plan for applying that knowledge is the key to maximizing your performance on test day. As your foundation of content knowledge is built up and strengthened, you'll find that the strategies included in this chapter become more and more effective in helping you quickly sift through the distractions and traps of the test to isolate the correct answer.

Now that you're preparing to move forward into the test content chapters of this book, be sure to keep your goal in mind. As you read, think about how you will be able to apply this information on the test. If you've already seen sample questions for the test and you have an idea of the question format and style, try to come up with questions of your own that you can answer based on what you're reading. This will give you valuable practice applying your knowledge in the same ways you can expect to on test day.

Good luck and good studying!

Basic Knowledge Associated with the Securities Industry

Purpose of the Marketplace

Self-Regulatory Organization

A self-regulatory organization, or SRO, is an organization that is established outside of the federal government to oversee an industry through the establishment of regulations and industry standards. The goal of the SROs with oversight of the securities industry is to protect investors through the creation of rules that encourage companies to conduct business fairly. The SROs that are responsible for the securities industry are subject to the jurisdiction of the Securities Exchange Commission, or the SEC. The SEC is a regulatory organization (part of the federal government) as opposed to a self-regulatory organization. Securities companies that subject themselves to the oversight of SROs are less likely to run afoul of federal laws.

The largest and most involved SROs in the securities industry are the Financial Industry Regulatory Authority (FINRA), the Municipal Securities Rule Making Board (MSRB), and the Chicago Board of Options Exchange (CBOE).

Financial Industry Regulatory Authority

FINRA (Financial Industry Regulatory Authority) has regulatory authority over all issues pertaining to investment banking (the underwriting of securities), over-the-counter trading, trading on the New York Stock Exchange, and any firm or individual that is a member of FINRA. FINRA also has oversight of investment companies (mutual fund companies, etc.) and transactions in which limited partnerships are traded. FINRA seeks to promote the securities industry and investment banking through the establishment of standardized practices and ethical standards by which business is conducted within those industries. These policies assist member firms in meeting local, state, and federal laws pertaining to the securities industry. FINRA also endeavors to facilitate communication among the member firms, and between FINRA members and the government. FINRA encourages self-discipline in its membership and may investigate and bring closure to disputes between members of FINRA, and between members of FINRA and the general investing public.

Securities and Exchange Commission

The Securities and Exchange Commission (SEC) is an agency of the US federal government which is primarily responsible for the regulation of the securities industry and stock and options exchanges. It was formed in 1934 by Franklin D. Roosevelt during the Great Depression. The SEC has the authority to file civil and criminal suits against those who violate SEC rules. All broker-dealers are required to register with the SEC.

SEC Act of 1934

The Securities Exchange Act of 1934 is the foundational law of American stock trading. After the 1929 stock market crash, many critics blamed the crash and subsequent depression on rampant speculation in an unregulated stock trading atmosphere, including selling short, buying on margin, and selling on margin. In response, the Congress passed the SEC Act, which established rules and regulations for stock trading in America, including the formation of the Securities and Exchange Commission (SEC) to enforce those laws.

In addition to creating the Securities and Exchange Commission, the SEC Act of 1934 requires that stock exchanges file their registration papers with the SEC, and requires any companies that trade on the exchanges to file their registration papers. It also established capital requirements and set rigid limits on borrowing and lending for purposes of buying on margin. It set rules governing insider trading and created general rules for trading stocks and other securities, including how customer accounts are handled, and the "customer protection rule." In addition, it set standards for ownership and administration of exchanges and broker firms.

Regulatory Organization

A regulatory organization is an organization that has been established by the federal government with oversight of a particular industry. The role of the regulatory organization is to create regulations to ensure fair and proper business dealings, and enforce those regulations. Regulatory organizations differ from self-regulatory organizations (SROs) in that SROs are established to encourage self-regulation within an industry. SROs and regulatory organizations work in concert to reduce federal intervention in industry. SROs usually fall under the oversight of the coinciding regulatory industry. The Securities Exchange Commission (SEC) is the regulatory organization with jurisdiction over the securities industry. The SEC works with FINRA, the securities industry SRO, to ensure compliance with federal regulation and reduce intervention by the SEC.

Securities Markets

The three types of securities markets are the primary market, the secondary market, and the over-the-counter market. The primary market is the market in which securities are sold by the issuers to investors. This is the market on which initial public offerings, or IPOs, are made. Retail investors typically do not participate in the primary market. Instead, they participate in the secondary market, in which securities that have already undergone underwriting and the initial public offering process are traded. This occurs on stock exchanges. Examples of the secondary market include the New York Stock Exchange (NYSE) and the American Stock Exchange (ASE). The third type of securities market is over-the-counter markets, or OTC markets. In OTC markets, trades are executed between individual parties without the oversight of a regulated exchange like the NYSE or the ASE. The best-known example of an OTC market is the NASDAQ.

Characteristics of Securities and Products

Private and Public Securities Offerings

A private securities offering need not undergo the vetting process of an initial public offering, as would a public offering, because it is not offered to the general public. While public offerings are sold to the investing public, private offerings are sold only to a very specific group, and the issuer may not solicit the investing public with their offering. There tend to be fewer regulations (therefore greater risk) of private offerings since they are not offered to the general public. Public offerings must submit to the registration requirements outlined in the Securities Act of 1933, whereas private offerings are exempt from such registrations. This is again due to the fact that private offerings are not made to the public. Private offerings are not as efficient at raising capital as public offerings, since they do not have access to the general investing public. This results in many of their investors being large institutions or groups of wealthy people with common investing goals.

Initial Public Offerings and Secondary Offerings

Initial public offerings, or IPOs, are securities offerings that have undergone the underwriting process and obtained registration. The proceeds of the IPO go to the issuing company. This method is often used to obtain capital to expand operations. A secondary offering is an offering in which a large number of issue shares are sold by major stockholders in a company. In a secondary offering, all of the proceeds go to the stockholders and are not usually used to expand company operations. Another type of offering, called a "shelf offering," displays characteristics of initial offerings but occurs after the initial public offering. In a shelf offering, the company selling the securities has already made an IPO of their company, but chose not to sell all of the shares in the IPO. Their SEC registrations are valid for two years, and they may sell the unsold securities for up to three years. In a shelf offering, the proceeds go to the issuing company.

Exempt and Non-Exempt Securities

Under the Securities Act of 1933, securities that are offered to the public must be registered with the Securities Exchange Commission, or SEC. Before a company may issue an initial public offering (IPO), they must submit to the registration process because they are not exempt from the requirements of the Securities Act of 1933. Therefore, a security that must submit to the registration process is called a non-exempt security.

There are certain types of securities that do not have to be registered with the SEC before being sold to the public. Since these securities are exempt from registration, there are referred to as exempt securities. Although exempt securities are exempt from registration under the Securities Act of 1933, they are not exempt from the anti-fraud portions of the act. The most common exempt securities are offering of the United States government, and offerings of United States municipalities.

Securities Exempted from Registration

Some securities are exempt from the registration requirements applicable to other securities per the Securities Act of 1933. This is due either to the credit standing of the issuer, which is perceived to be high, or to the authority belonging to a government regulatory agency. (In the case of fixed annuities, they are exempt because the insurance company guarantees them.) The exempt securities include the following:

- securities issued by the federal government or its agencies
- municipal (local government) bonds
- securities from banks, savings institutions, and credit unions
- public utility securities
- securities issued by nonprofit, educational, or religious institutions
- fixed annuities and insurance policies
- notes, bills of exchange, bankers' acceptances, and commercial paper with an initial maturity of at most 270 days

Transactions Exempted from Registration

In addition to specific securities being exempted from ordinary registration requirements, certain transactions can be exempted as well, including the following:

- intrastate offerings
- Regulation A offerings
- Regulation D offerings
- Regulation S offerings
- private (non-public) offerings

Registered and Unregistered Securities

When a corporation decides to make a public offering of their stock, they must undergo an underwriting process whereby they submit to all registration rules and processes required by the Securities Exchange Commission (SEC). This registration requirement by the SEC is in place to prevent abuse of public investors and ensure that the issuer is practicing business ethically (in regards to the issue). The registration process is lengthy and complex.

An unregistered security is a security that has not undergone the underwriting process. While it is generally illegal to sell unregistered securities, there are some exceptions to the rule. Regulations A and D and Rule 147 provide for the sale of partially registered or unregistered securities.

Exemptions from Registration That Regulations A and D and Rule 147 Provide for Securities

Regulation A provides for the partial registration of small offerings. A small offering is defined as an offering of five million dollars or less in a year's time. Registration is completed by filing a notice of sale with the Securities Exchange Commission (SEC) instead of the full registration process, which can be cost prohibitive to small companies.

Regulation D provides an exemption from regulation for issues of securities that are only offered by certain investors, and not to the general investing public. Since the public is not at risk in these offerings, registration with the SEC is not required. Private placements may only be sold to accredited investors or thirty-five or fewer non-accredited investors. Since private placements tend to be large, they're usually only available to institutional investors or groups of very wealthy individuals.

Rule 147 exempts intrastate offerings from SEC registration as long the purchasers of the issue reside in the state, 80% of the company's income is in-state, 80% of its assets are in-state, 80% of the proceeds from the issue are used in-state, and the underwriter is in-state.

Order of Liquidation Priority

If a corporation cannot meet its obligations, a bankruptcy court may order the liquidation of its assets to pay the debtors of the company. The order of liquidation describes who must be made whole first. Those coming after the first debtors may not receive all of the money owed them. In order from top priority to least priority are: workers' unpaid wages, taxes owed, secured claims (such as mortgages), secured liabilities (bonds issued), primary unsecured liabilities (bonds without collateral, debentures, general creditors), secondary unsecured liabilities, preferred stock holders, and common stockholders.

SIPC and FDIC

The SIPC (Securities Investor Protection Corporation) is a corporation created by the federal government that was established to protect the invested assets of an investor in the event that a broker/dealer declared bankruptcy. The SIPC protects up to $500,000 of the client's cash and securities, but will only cover $250,000 in cash. If more than $250,000 in cash is held at a brokerage, the SIPC will cover only the first $250,000. All brokers, dealers, and broker/dealers that are registered in accordance with the Securities Exchange Act of 1934 must be members of the SIPC. The SIPC does not cover losses incurred in the markets, or fraud committed by a third party; it only covers losses due to broker/dealer failure or bankruptcy.

The FDIC (Federal Deposit Insurance Corporation) covers losses incurred similarly through bank failure. The FDIC, however, only covers cash on deposit with banks. As such, the FDIC covers bank certificates of deposits (CDs), but not necessarily brokerages CDs. FDIC coverage should never be implied with investments.

Product Characteristics

Equities

Equities represent ownership in a company that has offered shares of that company for sale. Equities are represented by common stock and preferred stock. Common stock represents ownership in a company, and usually allows the holder to vote on new board members and changes or additions to corporate policy. Preferred stock represents ownership in a company, but these stockholders do not receive voting rights. Preferred stockholders do, however, tend to receive a regular dividend.

While the volatility of equities tends to provide more growth than other types of investments, the same volatility can result in larger losses. Volatility is more characteristic of common stock than preferred stock. This advantage in growth comes at a price, however. In the event of corporate liquidation, preferred stockholders receive their investments after everyone (other than common stockholders) receive their portion, and common stockholders are made whole subsequently. This can lead to equities holders not receiving all or any of their investment.

Authorized Stock, Issued Stock, and Outstanding Stock

Authorized stock is the maximum number of shares that a company has been approved to sell on the market. They may sell them all immediately, or hold them back for sale at a later date, or for other purposes, such as employee stock options. Holding stocks back is fairly common, and authorized shares often exceed the actual shares issued for sale on the market. Once all authorized shares have been sold, or issued, the company may not sell any more shares without getting approval from current stockholders, because the company charter must be amended.

Issued stock is the number of shares that have ever been sold and held, even if they have since been repurchased by the company or retired.

Outstanding stock is the number of shares that are currently held by investors and tradeable in the market. If no shares have been repurchased or retired, then issued stock = outstanding stock.

Treasury Stock

Shares that have been issued and sold are sometimes bought back by the company. The stock that is bought back from the market and held by the company is known as treasury stock. The corporation may hold the stock for future use, such as employee stock options, or they may retire it for good. Stock buybacks are usually seen as an indicator of a company's belief in the strength of its value, and are often followed by an increase in share value, as investors will interpret the buyback as a sign of strength. Even if the share price remains the same, the earning per share should go up, since the number of shares outstanding that will share in company earnings has been reduced. The rights that apply to outstanding stock still on the market, such as voting rights and dividend rights, don't apply to treasury stock.

Par Value for Stocks

The par value for a stock is the valued stated on the stock certificate. This is the requirement which the company is legally obligated to pay a shareholder in exchange for ownership in the company, no matter how worthless the stock certificate might be on the open market. Consequently, the par value for stocks tends to be very low, $1 or even $0.01 per share, in order to lower the company's obligation in the event of stock devaluation. Predictably, stocks with a par value are known as *par value stocks*, and stocks lacking a par value are known as *no par value stocks*.

Limited Liability

In sole proprietorships or partnerships, the owners of the business are fully responsible for the liabilities which their business incurs to various creditors. There is a connection between the assets they personally own and their business, so that if their business goes under, creditors can lay claim to other assets besides what they have invested in the business. This is *unlimited liability*.

By contrast, limited liability entails that investors are not liable for all of the debts which a corporation has, but are liable only to the extent of their investment. While investors can then partake of the benefits of the company's growth, they are not subject to enormous harm if the company has severe debts or even bankruptcy.

Stock Certificate

A stock certificate is a piece of paper stating how many shares of the stock a person owns. It also includes the name of the company, the investor's name, and the CUSIP number. CUSIP stands for Committee on Uniform Securities Identification Procedures. This is a unique identifier of stocks and bonds, much like a serial number, and it can be used to identify the rightful owner of these instruments if they're lost or stolen. To sell stocks, the owner of the shares must sign the back of the certificate, or a stock power, giving the right to his broker to make the transfer.

Preemptive Rights

A preemptive right is the right of a shareholder (though not of just any shareholder) to maintain his current percentage of share ownership in case the corporation decides to issue more stock. If a company decides to issue more stock, the company must give these privileged shareholders first crack at buying the shares before the company offers the shares to the general market (and usually below market price). Current shareholders will receive a subscription rights certificate, which will spell out the terms and conditions of the offer, such as the date, price, and how many shares they're entitled to buy based on their current ownership.

Rights of Common Stockholders

Common stockholders can have varying rights associated with their stock ownership. They can have *preemptive rights*, which privilege them to purchase shares of a new offering before the public; they can have a *pro rata share of dividends*, in which they receive dividends proportionally to their stock ownership in the corporation; they can have *access to corporate books*, where they gain information about the corporation's operations to which the public (and other shareholders) are not privy; and they can have various *voting powers* to influence the direction of the corporation.

Voting Powers for Common Stockholders

Common stockholders can have varying levels of voting powers. While most preferred stock does not include voting rights, most common stock does.

- Common stockholders generally get one vote for each share they own per issue to be decided. For instance, a stockholder owning 1,000 shares in a corporation, voting for candidates to fill 5 different positions on the board of directors, will have a total of 5,000 votes to expend. However, corporations can facilitate different kinds of voting, which explain how these votes can be expended.
- *Statutory voting* requires the stockholder to split up his votes evenly among the issues being voted on. For instance, the above shareholder will have 1000 votes maximum to expend on each of the 5 different positions being filled.
- *Cumulative voting*, on the other hand, does not require stockholders to split up their votes evenly. They are free to distribute their votes as they please. For instance, the above shareholder, if he wanted, could use all 5,000 of his votes on one particular candidate running for a singular position on the board of directors.
- Since it is often inconvenient for all common stockholders to physically attend annual corporate meetings, they can still exercise their voting rights by hiring *proxies*, agents legally enabled to vote on the stockholders' behalf.

Dividend

A dividend is a portion of the company's profit that is returned to shareholders. A dividend can come in the form of cash, in which case a check is sent to the owner or to the owner's brokerage account. When the company announces dividends, there will be some dollar amount per share distributed to shareholders. When dividends are paid in cash, they are considered income, and taxes must be paid on them during the tax year they're received.

Dividends can also be in the form of additional shares of stock given to shareholders. These are not taxable until they're sold, just like all stocks. Because this type of stock dividend increases the number of outstanding shares, it decreases the market value of each share, but does not affect the total market value of the company.

A corporation must let the stock exchange know that it is getting ready to pay a dividend. The day it announces this is the *declaration date*. When it makes this announcement, it will declare a *record date* and a *payment date*. The record date must be at least ten days after the declaration date. Whoever is the owner of record of shares on the record date will be entitled to the dividend. To be considered the owner of record, a stock buyer must purchase the stock before the ex-date, which is two days before the record date. In other words, the owner must purchase the stock at least three business days before the record date. The payment date is generally three to four weeks after the record date.

Penny Stocks

Penny stocks are shares of very small publicly traded companies, generally traded as over-the-counter stocks, not on major exchanges. These stocks are prone to speculative and volatile price changes and manipulation, thus being very risky. They are also characterized by illiquidity; that is, they are difficult to trade to others. Because of this, a broker must acquire his customer's written consent before facilitating any penny stock transactions for him.

There are special rules accompanying penny stock transactions. A broker wishing to facilitate such a transaction is required by the SEC to give the customer a document outlining the risks of penny stock investments, the market price for the stock, and the compensation the brokerage firm will receive for executing the transaction. Brokerage firms also must send monthly statements to penny stock investors, disclosing the value of their penny stocks.

Common Stock and Preferred Stock

The vast majority of stocks issued are common stock. Some corporations issue a limited number of preferred stocks. Holders of preferred stock do not have voting rights under most circumstances. But there are financial benefits to owning preferred stock instead of common stock. If a company goes bankrupt, preferred stock owners take precedence over common stock holders when it comes to distributing whatever assets are available. And preferred stock usually comes with a fixed dividend paid on a regular basis, so that even if the owners of common stock don't receive a dividend, preferred stock owners will. And because the dividend is fixed, owners of preferred stock can depend on a regular income. Because of these differences, the prices of preferred stocks tend to rise and fall with relation to interest rates, and not with other factors that affect the price of the common stock.

Cumulative Preferred Stock and Participating Preferred Stock

Cumulative preferred stock is preferred stock that gives the stockholder the right to missed dividend payments from the company. Should the company miss a dividend payment to owners of cumulative preferred stock, the company must make up the payment at a later date, as it stays on the books as a debt until paid. This is opposed to *straight (or non-cumulative) preferred stock*, which has a fixed dividend payment (like cumulative preferred stock), but if the company misses any payments, they are not made up later.

Participating preferred stock entitles the stockholder to a portion of the profits that remain after dividends and interest have been paid by the corporation. These are so called because they permit stockholders to participate further in the company's profits. Participating preferred stockholders also have special rights should the corporation liquidate.

Convertible Preferred Stock and Callable Preferred Stock

Convertible preferred stock consists of shares that can be converted into common stock if the owner so chooses. The conversion price is preset, and convertible preferred shares tend to rise and fall in value along with common shares because of this feature. They also usually have lower dividend payments than other preferred stocks.

Callable preferred stock consists of shares that the company reserves the right to buy back at a future date at a specific price. When a company calls a preferred share, it will pay a premium over the stated price to make up for loss of future dividends. This can also be called *redeemable preferred stock*. Callable preferred stock is ordinarily covered by a *sinking fund provision*. In the same way that corporations can repurchase bonds with a sinking fund, the same can be done for their repurchasing of preferred stock.

Debt Securities and Fixed-Income Securities

Debt securities generally fall into the fixed-income category, although not all are fixed-income. Debt securities are securities issued as debt of a company, and that debt is sold to investors. The most common type of debt security is a bond. Most bonds pay a fixed amount of interest to an investor and fall into the fixed income category. However, some bonds, called zero coupon bonds, do not pay interest and are not fixed income securities. Debt securities are one of the first creditors to receive money owed to them in the event of corporate liquidation.

Bonds that pay interest are fixed-income securities. Other types of fixed income securities can include preferred stock, real-estate investment trusts (REITs), certificates of deposit, and many more. Fixed-income securities are characterized by low volatility. They do not typically suffer (or benefit) from large value swings as do common stocks.

Bond

A bond is a debt instrument, or debt security. Unlike stockowners, investors who purchase bonds receive no ownership in the company and no voting rights. Bonds are issued by private companies, by the federal government, and by state and local governments (municipal bonds) to raise money for various projects, or for operating expenses. The value of bonds fluctuates with interest rates, and not with the success of the company or the stock market. Should a company go bankrupt, bond owners are compensated before stockholders if there are any assets to be liquidated. For this reason, bonds are called senior securities.

Term Bonds and Serial Bonds

Any particular bond always has a particular maturity date, but bond issuers can attempt to strategically issue bonds of different durations for the sake of financing their own activities. Term bonds are bonds of the same issuance which have the same maturity date, whereas serial bonds mature at different (though regular) intervals.

Yield to Maturity, Yield to Call, and Yield to Worst

A bond's yield to maturity (YTM) is how much return the bondholder will earn annually by holding the bond all the way to its maturity date. If it is the original owner of the bond, this is the coupon rate, or nominal yield. But if the bondholder bought the bond on the market, the yield to maturity (YTM) will depend on whether he bought the bond at a discount or at a premium. (Very few bonds trade at par.) Bonds bought at a discount will have a higher YTM, and bonds bought at a premium will have a lower YTM. Yield to maturity is also called *basis*.

Yield to call (YTC) is the bondholder's return if the bond is called before it matures.

Yield to worst (YTW) is the lowest possible yield for a bond without the issuer defaulting. It is obtained by calculating the YTM and the YTC for all the call dates and selecting the lowest.

Discount Yield

The discount yield of a bond is the return to a bondholder for short-term bonds and T-bills sold at a discount. The calculation for discount yield assumes 30-day durations for months and 360-day durations for years.

Bond Indentures

For any bond, the interest rate, frequency of interest payments, maturity date, characteristics of the bond (e.g. convertibility, callability), and the principal amount need to be disclosed in a contract between the bond issuer and the bond buyer. This contract is called an indenture.

Call Provisions

Call provisions are arrangements on bonds stating that the bond issuer has the right to purchase back and retire the bond. These provisions ordinarily establish a timeframe when the call can occur, including details on the price and accrued interest paid to the bondholders. Bond issuers will call bonds if the market interest rate is lower than the bond rate, so that they can refinance their bonds to pay less interest. Due to the risk this places on bond investors, bonds with call provisions have a higher yield.

A particular type of call provision is a *make whole call*, whose aim is to properly compensate bond investors for future interest revenues they do not receive because of a bond call. With a make whole call provision, the bond issuer will be required to pay a lump sum equal to the net present value (NPV) of the future interest payments at the time of the call.

Convertible Bonds

Convertible bonds are bonds that can be converted into a stated amount of shares of the issuing company's stock. This makes them attractive to investors because they combine features of both financial instruments—they pay interest, which is regular income, and they can also appreciate if the company's stock appreciates. If the stock goes up, the holder of a convertible bond can choose to convert them to stocks, or sell the bond on the market, and receive a premium to reflect the appreciation of the stock.

Some convertible bonds give the issuer the right to *force conversions*, forcing bondholders to convert their convertible bonds into stock. Companies who force conversions usually do so to refinance their bonds if a lower interest rate is available.

Bond Refunding and Pre-Refunding

Bond refunding is when an issuer sells a new bond issue in order to raise money to redeem a previous bond issue. This is done to take advantage of lower interest rates. Refunding becomes more likely as bonds get closer to the maturity date.

Pre-refunding is when the issuer sells a new set of bonds at a lower interest rate, but doesn't call the previous issue of bonds. The proceeds from the sale are placed in escrow and used to buy federal government securities, and the interest received is used to call the previous issue at the first call date. This is also known as *advance refunding*. Bonds that are pre-refunded have the highest possible bond rating, as the risk of default is virtually nil.

Factors That Affect a Bond's Liquidity

The following affect bond liquidity:

- how well-known or widely owned they are
- the bond rating (higher rating → easier trades)
- the quality of the bond issuer
- how mature the bond is
- how high the interest rate is
- whether it is trading at, above, or below par
- whether it has any call features

Bank Qualified Bonds

Banks like the benefit of tax-exempt interest earned on municipal bonds. But with the Tax Reform Act of 1986, banks can't deduct the carrying cost of holding municipal bonds in inventory; that is, they can't deduct the interest expenses which are incurred to purchase or carry those bonds. This tends to negate the benefits of tax-exempt interest income.

But there are exceptions to this rule which allow banks to deduct 80% of the carrying cost on particular bonds. Specifically, if the bonds are issued by a qualified small issuer (i.e. an issuer that issues $10 million in tax-exempt bonds or less yearly), issued for some public purpose, and designated as tax-exempt, then they qualify. These types of bonds are often called bank qualified bonds.

Treasury Bonds

Treasury bonds (T-bonds) are long-term obligations issued by the United States Treasury Department of the federal government. The proceeds from them help fund the long-term operations of the federal government. Like T-notes, T-bonds pay interest every six months. They are issued with maturities of ten to thirty years. For five years, from 2001 to 2006, the federal government stopped issuing thirty-year bonds. But due to popular demand by investors, the sale of thirty-year bonds was re-instituted in January of 2006. They are quoted as a percentage of par in 1/32 increments.

Gains from Treasury bonds are taxed only at the federal level.

Treasury Bills

Treasury Bills (T-bills) are short-term obligations issued by the United States Treasury Department of the federal government. Like zero-coupon bonds, they don't pay interest, but are sold at less than face value, and the buyer collects face value at maturity. They are one of the main ways of funding the operation of the federal government, and they are sold in amounts ranging from $1,000 to $1,000,000. They have maturities of 4, 13, or 26 weeks. Their prices are quoted in yield, which means that on paper the bid will be higher than the ask.

Gains from Treasury bills are taxed only at the federal level.

Treasury Notes

Treasury notes (T-notes) are medium-term obligations issued by the United States Treasury Department of the federal government. Unlike T-bills, Treasury notes do pay interest, paying every six months. Proceeds from Treasury notes are used to fund the intermediate operations of the federal government. Their maturities range from one to ten years. They may also be refunded at maturity, with a new note instead of payment. T-notes are quoted as a percentage of par in increments of 1/32.

Gains from Treasury notes are taxed only at the federal level.

Collateralized Mortgage Obligations

Collateralized mortgage obligations (CMOs) are issued by private financial institutions. They are bundles of private mortgages, much like the pass-throughs that are put together by the various federal agencies. Although marketed by private companies, CMOs are usually secured with financial instruments from Ginnie Mae, Freddie Mac, and Fannie Mae, and so are rated AAA.

Mortgages are bundled by maturity dates into groups called *tranches*. In a standard CMO, all tranches receive interest payments every month, but only one tranche at a time receives principal payments.

Collateralized Debt Obligations

Collateralized debt obligations (CDOs) are similar to CMOs, also being subdivided into tranches bearing different degrees of risks and maturities. The main difference is that they are backed by debts other than mortgages, such as loans or bonds.

Derivatives

Derivatives are investments that derive their value from another security's value, thus the term "derivative." The most common types of derivatives are futures and forward contracts, and options. Futures and forward contracts are contracts that are traded based on the current or expected price of a commodity. Options are contracts that give the investor the option of buying or selling a security at a set price. The fluctuations of the value of the underlying security of an option cause the value of the option to fluctuate as well.

Depending upon the underlying security, derivatives can display a high degree of stability or a high degree of volatility. The term derivative covers such a broad spectrum of investments that very few derivatives share characteristics, other than their value being based upon an underlying security. Derivatives have many uses for investors. Some use them to generate income without taking much risk, while others may use them to take on a great deal of risk in return for the possibility of great reward. Still others may use them for a hedge against market volatility.

Open-Ended Mutual Funds

Mutual funds are investments that are offered by investment companies that constantly offer new shares of an investment portfolio; they're often referred to as open-ended. Investors that purchase shares of mutual funds participate in gains and losses proportionate to their investment. Mutual fund holders may sell (or redeem) their positions in the fund at the end of the trading day. Mutual funds are redeemed at net asset value, or NAV, which is calculated at the end of each trading day based on the underlying holdings of the mutual fund.

Mutual funds can serve many purposes. The underlying securities of a mutual fund determine the purpose of the fund. If the fund is made up of bonds, it's likely that the intent of the mutual fund is to provide exposure to the bond market in a more convenient method than holding traditional bonds. The same can be said of a fund that is made up of equities. Mutual funds are useful to nearly every investor, as there are so many different types of mutual funds with different objectives.

Variable Annuities

Variable annuities are insurance products that guarantee an investor a stream of income based upon an account value. Variable annuities are funded with premium payments similar to life insurance, but the premiums are allowed exposure to market movement. This allows the investor access to the market to help their investment grow, while still offering annuity features. Modern variable annuity products offer guarantees of account values from which the investor may take income. Variable annuities tend to come with high fees and pay high commissions to those selling them. As such, they have gained a bad reputation despite their usefulness. An investor seeking income within ten to fifteen years might find that a variable annuity is very useful in providing a guaranteed income amount while providing access to the growth of the securities markets.

Real Estate Investment Trusts

Real estate investment trusts are organizations that invest a pool of capital, provided by multiple investors, to invest in real estate that provides income. Occasionally, REITs will also purchase mortgage loans and take the interest payments as income. REITs are usually organized as a trust that allows them to benefit from Subchapter M of the Internal Revenue Code. Subchapter M allows the trust to avoid being taxed as a corporation if at least 75% of their holdings are in real estate, with 75% of their income coming from rents received or mortgage interest, and if they distribute at least 90% of their net investment income to shareholders. REITs are usually useful to those seeking income, but have enough of a time horizon to be able to hold the REITs for four to ten years. This often makes REITs unsuitable as a large portion of a portfolio, as they tend to be illiquid investments.

Exchange Traded Funds

Exchange traded funds are shares of portfolios that are issued by investment companies, and then traded on exchanges like an individual stock. They are similar to mutual funds in that the value of the security is based upon the underlying holdings, but unlike mutual funds, once the shares have been offered, no more shares are created. This has led to ETFs being referred to as closed end funds.

The underlying portfolios of ETFs can be varied and far-reaching. An ETF may hold a basket of bonds, precious metals, commodities, stocks from emerging economies, and a multitude of other securities. This makes them very useful to investors in that can fill a need in a portfolio without the inconvenience of conventional investment methods, such as storing precious metals after purchase.

Basic Knowledge of Broker/Dealer Characteristics

Broker/Dealer

A broker/dealer is an individual or company that buys and sells securities as a business. A broker/dealer can act as both agent (placing a transaction for a client) and principal (dealing from their own inventory for profit), but not both in the same transaction. This is to prevent double-charging investors since broker/dealers are compensated by charging a commission when they act as brokers and charging a markup when they act as dealers.

Broker/dealers are required to register with the Securities Exchange Commission (SEC), self-regulatory organizations, and states where they transact business. Broker/dealers help facilitate the flow of trading by filling orders from their own inventory (and sometime buying for their own inventory), and by finding a buyer or seller when they do not have the inventory that an investor wishes to buy.

Registered Investment Advisor

According to the Investment Advisors Act of 1940, a Registered Investment Advisor is a "person or firm that, for compensation, is engaged in the act of providing advice, making recommendations, issuing reports or furnishing analyses on securities, either directly or through publications," and is registered with the Securities Exchange Commission, or SEC. Registration with the SEC is only registration and should not be presented as an endorsement from the government regulator.

Registered Investment Advisors, or RIAs, have a fiduciary responsibility to their clients and must always act in the best interest of the client. RIAs differ from broker/dealers in their method of practicing business. A broker/dealer has no responsibility to ensure that all of its clients' purchases and sells are suitable to the client's best interest. Broker/dealers act in their own interest, while RIAs must legally and ethically act in the best interest of the client.

Suitability

Suitability is a vitally important concept that applies to each investor regardless of their time, net worth, liquidity needs, etc. Determining the suitability of an investment is a process by which the advisor analyzes the client's assets, goals, and needs and determines which investments are best for that client. An illiquid real-estate portfolio might not be suitable for someone that requires liquidity and has limited assets, but for a larger investor for whom liquidity is not an issue, and they desire real-estate exposure, that same portfolio is probably suitable.

With the advisor's fiduciary responsibility comes the responsibility to ensure that each investment is suitable to the client. The suitability of an investment should be determined without regard to the compensation that is given to the advisor; if compensation is considered when making a recommendation, the advisor's fiduciary responsibility has been violated.

Compensation

Advisors are usually compensated in one of two ways. Advisors may receive a commission from a security sold (usually in the form of a percentage of the total sale or buy), or they may charge a client a fee to manage their assets. For advisors to continue to be compensated under a commission arrangement, they must continue to sell products to clients. This can occasionally lead to ethical challenges, as an advisor may choose to sell a product to a client that is less suitable than another investment that is more suitable, but compensates the advisor with less commission.

Fee based relationships are arrangements by which the advisor is compensated with a set annual fee. Fee based arrangements allow the advisor to continue to receive compensation for advice given without additional securities being sold. They also remove (for the most part) the temptation for the advisor to sell the highest commission product, since they do not receive commission.

Statement and Performance Report

A client statement is simply a statement of the client's assets held with a particular company. They contain hard data regarding amounts and values of holdings. Statements of account do not provide performance measures unless they are combined with a performance report. Firms are required to send a quarterly statement (or a more often statement) that displays the activity that has occurred in the account since the last statement was sent, all securities positions, and account balances.

A performance report is simply a report with measures of the performance of the client's holdings. These reports are not required by law, but many firms send them out to provide value to their clients.

REGULATORY REQUIREMENTS OF BROKER/DEALERS

FINANCIAL AND OPERATIONS PRINCIPAL

Rule G-27 of the Municipal Securities Rulemaking Board (MSRB) states that all municipal securities firms are required to employ a principal to oversee the company's representatives, and to write and maintain a written manual of supervisory procedures. Further among the responsibilities of the financial and operations principal, or FinOp, are to approve or reject (in writing) the opening of new accounts, approve or reject in writing all municipal securities transactions, approve or reject in writing steps taken to resolve client complaints, and approve or reject in writing correspondence pertaining to the trading of municipal securities. All broker/dealers (not including bank dealers) must employ FinOps to keep financial records and books.

FINANCIAL AND OPERATIONAL COMBINED UNIFORM SINGLE REPORT

The Financial and Operational Combined Uniform Single (FOCUS)report is a report pertaining to operational and financial issues that all stock exchanges must file with the Securities Exchange Commission, or SEC. They must file the report monthly and quarterly. Broker/dealers must also file the reports with their self-regulatory organization (SRO), usually FINRA. The FOCUS report includes information about a firm's cash, securities, and liquid asset positions. This report helps the SRO determine whether the firm is healthy enough to continue business. The FOCUS report also aides in identifying firms that may need counseling to prevent them from becoming unstable and possibly unfit to continue business.

GENERAL LEDGER

A firm's general ledger is an accounting record by which records of all of the firm's transactions are kept. The general ledger is typically the source document from which reports such as financial statements originate. General ledgers also contain information about the firm's income, assets, liabilities, owners' equity, expenses, etc. Such information is very useful to an investor considering buying equity in a firm, and can be an indicator of the health of the firm.

Broker/dealers' general ledgers are subject to scrutiny by self-regulatory organizations (usually FINRA) to ensure that consumers' funds are not at risk due to poor management of the broker/dealer.

NET CAPITAL

Net capital is a measurement of company's asset and liabilities. It is determined with the following equation: $net\ capital = liquid\ assets - total\ liabilities$. Net capital is similar to an individual's liquid net worth, but it differs in that net worth includes all assets whereas net capital only includes liquid assets. Illiquid assets, such as real estate, are not included in the net capital calculation. All companies that are members of the Financial Industry Regulatory Authority (FINRA) must submit to net capital requirements, or a minimum of net capital. The minimum net capital requirements are in place to guarantee that members have sufficient capital to meet financial obligations to their clients and to other FINRA members. If a firm takes more risk than usual, their net capital requirement will be higher than usual to ensure that they can meet those financial obligations.

Reserve Requirement

A carrying firm that is a member of the Financial Industry Regulatory Authority (FINRA) must make a weekly calculation (at the close of business each Friday) to determine how much money the firm owes to clients, and how much money is owed to the firm by clients. This is accomplished by subtracting the money that the firm owes to clients from the money that is owed to the firm. If the amount that the firm owes is more than is owed to clients, the firm must deposit the difference into a reserve account that has been established for the purpose. The formula that describes the preceding would be as follows: *money owed to the firm – money owed to its clients = required reserve deposit.*

Types of Broker/Dealer Businesses

Executing Broker/Dealers and Prime Brokers

An executing broker/dealer is a broker/dealer that accepts and enters orders for clients. If that transaction is deemed to be "in good order," the executing broker/dealer will enter the trade on behalf of the client. Typically, the clients with whom they work are average retail investors. Prime broker is a term that refers to specialized services that some broker/dealers offer to select groups of clients, often high net-worth individuals, or HNIs. These specialized services can include cash management, securities lending, leveraged trade executions, and many other specialized services HNIs may require that an ordinary retail investor may not. Prime brokers and executing brokers often work together to service clients. Since the prime broker provides specialized services, they may facilitate the executing broker by clearing trades that the executing broker has placed on behalf of the client.

Clearing Broker/Dealer and an Introducing Broker/Dealer

An introducing broker/dealer is broker/dealer (BD) that does not retain a client's securities or cash, but instead "introduces" the client to a clearing broker/dealer. Introducing broker/dealers are not often large companies, and don't have the resources of a larger clearing broker/dealer, but they facilitate communication and connection between clearing broker/dealers and clients. Introducing BDs also direct transactions that they may not be able to execute to clearing broker/dealers.

The introducing BD's main role is to attract new assets, not necessarily to manage them. They often hold seminars and other informational events to attract clients, and perform other marketing roles. While the introducing BD is helpful to a clearing BD by bringing clients to them, the introducing BD cannot hold client funds or securities; thus, they are dependent upon the clearing BD. This situation is not reciprocal, however. Clearing BDs can operate independently of introducing BDs, but they benefit from increased transaction volumes that introducing BDs bring them.

Clearing Broker/Dealer and a Clearing Facility

A clearing broker/dealer is a broker/dealer (BD) that clears securities for their own transactions and provides the same services for other broker/dealers. They also provide record-keeping services associated with clearing. Clearing BDs may provide their services on a full-disclosure basis, in which they are fully aware of all information regarding the client that they are servicing, or on an omnibus basis, in which the only firms privy to the client's information is the other broker/dealer, not the clearing BD. A clearing facility is a firm that clears and settles transactions for other firms only. They do not have a brokerage division that executes transactions. All clearing done by a clearing facility is on behalf of others, not for themselves.

Institutional Investors and Institutional Trades

The term institutional investor typically refers to large companies that invest on behalf of a group of clients. Insurance companies, employee stock option plans, endowments, pension funds, private equity firms, venture capital firms, and 401k companies all fall under the definition of institutional investors. The Depository Trust and Clearing Corporation (DTCC) clears trades for institutional investors. Since institutional investors serve large numbers of investors, they typically make very large trades composed of millions of dollars in cash and securities per transaction. Settlement time for institutional trades is the same as retail trades. Most securities clear one day from the trade date, or T+1. Before the advent of automated clearing services, such as DTCC, the nature of such large trades made it difficult to settle institutional trades in such a short time.

Soft Dollars

"Soft dollars" are a form of compensation given to an investing firm wherein the firm that clears the transaction for the investment company gives them access to free research, order management systems, and professional subscriptions that would other cost the investment firm money. This is done in exchange for the investment firm sending the majority of their business to the clearing firm. The Securities Exchange Commission (SEC) disallows the use of soft dollars for physical goods such as computer equipment, coverage of travel costs, or overhead expenses. Soft dollar arrangements must be disclosed to clients. Both of the before-mentioned requirements must be met to ensure that the firm is acting in a legal and ethical manner.

Basic Knowledge Associated with Broker-Dealer Operations

Basic Knowledge of Account Opening and Maintenance

Retail, Institutional, and Prime Brokerage Customer Accounts

Retail Accounts

Retail accounts are investment accounts used by individual investors. Specifically, they are not for institutional investors. The individual owning the account does not necessarily need to be a natural person; trusts may own retail accounts. There are multiple types of retail accounts. Retail accounts may only have one owner, or they may have multiple owners. The persons owning the accounts may be natural or legal persons. Retail accounts are established for non-sophisticated investors and regulations are put in place in order to protect them from unethical investment professionals. As such retail accounts should be monitored for fraudulent activity and reviewed to ensure that investments in the accounts meet the clients' needs and goals.

Single-Owner Retail and the TOD Designation

Single-owner retail accounts are accounts that are owned by a single person, legal or natural. The only person that may initiate transactions and determine the movement of the securities in the account is the owner. In the case of trust ownership, the trustee of the trust may act in this manner. The TOD designation stands for *transfer on death*. This allows the account owner to name a beneficiary of the account that will receive the assets of the account and avoid probate courts. The TOD designation bypasses the estate; this allows the avoidance of probate. Money inherited through a TOD designation bypasses the estate, however, if the estate tax applies to the inherited money it will not bypass the estate tax. All inherited securities, whether by TOD or some other method, receive a "step-up" in basis. This means that the cost basis of the inherited securities is changed to the value of the securities on the date of the deceased's death.

Joint Accounts

A joint retail account is an investment account that is owned by more than one adult. Each owner has a specified amount of control over the account. Joint accounts must be established with a new account form and a joint account agreement, both of which must be signed by all owners.

The two types of joint accounts are *tenants in common* and *joint tenants with rights of survivorship.* The amount of control each owner has over the account depends upon the joint account type. Tenants-in-common accounts separate the interests in the account. If an owner passes away, their interest in the account passes to their estate. Accounts registered as joint tenants with rights of survivorship combine assets. At one of the owners' deaths, the entire amount of the account belongs to the remaining owners.

Partnership Accounts

A partnership is defined as an association of more than one person that is not incorporated. Typically, business owners open partnership accounts to meet specific goals; they may open cash accounts, margin accounts, retirement accounts, and other types of accounts that may help them achieve their goals. If a partnership chooses to open a margin account, they must disclose investment limitations.

In addition to a new account application, partnership accounts also require partnership agreements which outline who may transact business on the account. Partnership accounts tend to require more maintenance than average retail accounts because ownership tends to change in partnerships. With each change in a partnership, amended partnership agreements must be submitted.

Prime Brokerage Accounts

A prime brokerage account is an account, usually held by institutions, wherein the client chooses a member firm, a prime broker, to custody and finance their securities, and selects another firm, the executing broker, to handle the account's trading. The Securities Exchange Commission (SEC) requires that clients holding prime brokerage accounts must maintain a minimum balance of $500,000 in the account.

For prime brokerage accounts to be opened, the prime broker and account holder must sign an account agreement that outlines the terms of the agreement and names the executing broker or brokers. Additionally, the prime broker and executing broker or brokers must also sign a written agreement outlining the terms of the agreement between the brokers. Correspondence with the clients comes from the prime broker, while physical trading is performed by the executing broker.

Trading Authority on an Account by a Non-Owner

If the owners of an investment account wish for a third party to have trading authority on their account, they must grant that person power of attorney over the account. Power of attorney must be granted to a person in writing.

There are two types of authority granted with power of attorney. Limited powers of attorney give the third party, or attorney in fact, restricted access to the account. The power of attorney document outlines the specific powers that are granted to an attorney in fact with limited power of attorney. The other level of authority granted with the power of attorney document is full power of attorney. An individual with full power of attorney may transact on the account as if they were an owner. There are no restrictions outlined on the power of attorney document in this case. If the account owner or the attorney in fact passes away, the power of attorney document is voided.

Types of Individual and Employer Sponsored Retirement Accounts

Qualified and Non-Qualified Retirement Plans

There are all sorts of retirement plans, and they all have unique features. But one key feature that sets many of them apart from others is the fact that contributions to them are tax-deductible. Plans that feature tax-deductible contributions are known as qualified plans; the ones that don't are known as nonqualified plans. Two of the best-known nonqualified plans are payroll deduction plans and deferred compensation plans.

Nonqualified plans still benefit from tax-deferred growth. For qualified plans, distributions are taxed entirely as income, but for nonqualified plans, since the original contributions were from after-tax dollars, only the distributions in excess of the original contributions are taxed as income.

Individual Retirement Accounts

Individual Retirement Accounts (IRAs) are individual investment accounts that were created by legislation to incentivize people to prepare for retirement. Anyone with earned income may open and contribute to an IRA.

IRAs are attractive to investors because the earnings in the account grow on a tax-deferred basis, and contributions to IRAs are tax deductible until the income earned reaches a phase-out limit. Capital gains and dividends are not taxed until the investor starts taking distributions. A person may contribute only earned income to an IRA, and only a certain portion of that. As of 2026, an investor may contribute $7,500 to an IRA or $8,600 if the investor is over age 50. If an investor does not have $7,500 in earned income, they may only contribute up to the amount of income that is earned for the year.

Roth IRAs

A Roth IRA is an individual retirement account (IRA) that has distinct features from traditional IRAs. Roth IRA contributions may not be deducted on a tax return; this feature allows them to be distributed tax free when the investor begins taking distributions from the account. Only earned income may be contributed to a Roth IRA, and as of 2026, the contribution limit to a Roth IRA is $7,500 or $8,600 if the investor is age 50 or over. Income earners face phase out limits (of income earned) at which point they may no longer contribute to Roth IRAs.

Investors may not begin taking distributions from Roth IRAs until they are age 59½ and the money has been in the account for at least 5 years without being subject to tax and/or penalty. There are hardship reliefs from this rule, however. There is no penalty if the distribution is due to death, disability, or a first-time home purchase.

Rules Regarding Distributions from Individual Retirement Accounts

Since individual retirement accounts (IRAs) were established as an incentive for investors to save for retirement, rules discouraging early withdrawals from the account were written into the legislation establishing IRAs. Investors may not take distributions from the account until they reach age 59½. If they do begin taking distributions prior to this age, they will receive a 10% penalty on the amount withdrawn and be required to pay their earned income tax rate on the amount withdrawn. There are certain hardships for which this penalty is waived. Additionally, rule 72t of the Internal Revenue Code allows penalty free distributions before age 59½. Since contributions to IRAs are tax deductible, the IRS requires that individuals begin to take a required minimum distribution (RMD) by age 72. The RMD is calculated based on several factors, but the primary factor is the age of the investor.

EMPLOYER-SPONSORED RETIREMENT PLANS

There are two types of employer-sponsored retirement plans: defined contribution plans and defined benefit plans. Defined benefit plans are those plans put in place by employers to which the employee may not contribute. The employer contributes to the plan on behalf of the employee and gives the employee access to the plan assets upon retirement. The most common example of a defined benefit plan is a pension.

A define contribution plan is a savings plan in which the employee is allowed to contribution to the plan. The employer may or may not contribute as well. The attractive feature of defined contribution plans is that they are usually mobile between places of employment, whereas benefit plans are usually not. The most common type of defined contribution plan is a 401(k) in the for-profit sector and 403(b) in the non-profit sector.

401(K) PLANS, 403(B) PLANS, AND 457 PLANS

Most corporations now use 401(k) plans to fund their employee retirement pensions. With a 401(k), employees contribute a portion of their wages or salary, which are not counted as part of their gross income. Their contributions and the earnings on the contributions are tax deferred until withdrawal. In addition, the corporation may choose to match part of the employee's contribution. Most companies will have a variety of investment vehicles that an employee can choose to contribute to; the employee may put all his money in one or spread the money out among several.

403(b) plans are also called *tax-sheltered annuity (TSA) plans*. They are only available to people who work in educational institutions, including college, universities, elementary schools, middle schools, high schools, religious institutions, private hospitals, and institutions with an educational purpose, such as zoos and museums. In addition, the employees must be at least 21 years old, and must have at least one year of service before being eligible for coverage. The benefits of 403(b) plans are very similar to 401(k)s.

457 plans are nonqualified plans available to government employers (as well as certain non-government employers), similar in structure to 401(k)s and 403(b)s. They are deferred-compensation plans, and unlike 401(k)s and 403(b)s, they have no penalty on early distributions, even though distributions are taxed as income.

Keogh Plans (HR-10)

Keogh plans were established to assist self-employed persons and small businesses in providing retirement plans to their owners and employees. Keogh plans meet all ERISA requirements. Similar to IRAs, monies contributed to Keogh plans must be from earned income. The business that the Keogh plan covers must show a profit; if there is no profit earned, the business owner may not contribute to the Keogh plan. If a business is covered by a Keogh plan, the owner of the business may not discriminate as to who may participate in the plan. All full-time employees (those employees working at least 1,000 hours in a year) must be covered, unless they have not worked for the employer for at least a year and are under age 21.

Transferring a Retirement Plan and Rolling a Retirement Plan Over

An investor is allowed by law to transfer custodianship of their retirement funds. This is accomplished in one of two ways: transfers and rollovers.

A transfer occurs when the investor instructs the current custodian of their retirement account to close their retirement account and send the funds to another retirement account with a different custodian. An investor is allowed by law an unlimited number of transfers during a year as long as they do not physically take possession of the funds (i.e., check form). A rollover occurs when the investor physically receives funds from their retirement account, usually in check form, and then re-deposits it with another custodian. This deposit must occur within 60 days of receiving the distribution to qualify as a rollover instead of a distribution. An investor is only allowed one rollover per year per account.

ERISA

The acronym ERISA stands for Employee Retirement Income Security Act. ERISA is a piece of legislation that passed through Congress in 1974 to help protect the retirement savings of people in non-governmental jobs. ERISA was designed chiefly to ensure that corporations did not mismanage their employees' pension plans. It does so by outlining requirements that employers must follow such as who is allowed to participate, how the plan is funded and the investments that are in the plan, the period of time that it takes for an employee to be vested in the account, communication about the plan to the employees, nondiscrimination rules to ensure that all employees are treated equally and fairly, and by identifying parties-in-interest to the plan, or anyone that participates in or can affect the plan, such as the plan manager.

Permissible and Non-Permissible Investments and Holdings in an IRA

The only thing an investor is allowed to contribute (deposit) into an individual retirement account (IRA) is cash. While an investor may not deposit securities directly into their retirement account (this excludes transfers between retirement accounts), they may buy securities with the cash that they invest. Allowable securities include, but are not necessarily limited to stocks, bonds, investment company securities such as ETFs and mutual funds, and precious metal coins minted by the United States.

Investors may not purchase certain investments with their contributions such as rare stamps, antiques, artwork, precious gems, and rare coins. Additionally, life insurance may not be purchased in an IRA (this excludes annuity products). Given the risk inherent to margin accounts and the purpose of retirement accounts, margin accounts are not suitable accounts for retirement funds.

Account Opening

Entities That Are Permitted to Open and Transact Business in Investment Accounts

All persons, legal and natural, are permitted to open and transact in investment accounts. If a natural person, or individual, wishes to open an investment account for his or her own purposes they may do so, so long as they follow the guidelines and regulations regarding investment accounts. As long as all requirements are met, including completion of the new account paperwork, an individual may open and transact in as many investment accounts as they like.

Legal persons, or corporations, may also open and transact in investment accounts. In addition to the new account paperwork, corporations must also provide copies of the corporate charter (as proof that the corporation exists), and a corporate resolution bearing the corporate seal. The corporate resolution contains information about the persons or officers that are permitted to transact in the account.

Information That Must Be Present on New Account Paperwork

When opening a new investment account, extensive information must be gathered about the applying customer. The new account form must contain the following information to be in good order. The name and social security number (or tax ID if the applicant is a business) of each customer that has access to the account, the applying customers' dates of birth, their addresses, their business and home phone numbers, their occupation, for whom they work, and what type of business in which they work, what their country of citizenship is, their net worth and annual income, what they hope to accomplish through investing, whether the client is an employee of another member of FINRA, how they came to be a client of the firm, and the names and occupations of the persons allowed to transact on the account. After all of this information is gathered, the registered representative that opened the account must sign off on the account, and the representative principal or branch manager must sign off as well.

Standing Settlement Instructions

When the client establishes an account, they may designate a default option of settlement. They may alter the option for individual transactions, but if no instructions are given, the standing settlement instructions are used.

There are several different options for settlement. In the transfer and ship option, the registration of the securities are changed to that of the purchaser and delivered to them. The transfer and hold method changes the registration of the securities, but allows the broker/dealer to hold the securities for the purchaser. If a security is "held in street name," it means the security is registered to the broker/dealer and held by the broker/dealer, but the client is the actual owner. The delivery versus payment method of settlement is one in which the registered representative delivers the purchased securities to a bank for the client, and the bank pays for the securities on delivery.

Instances When Account Activity Can Be Restricted or Refused

Account activity can be restricted in different ways for different accounts.

- A mutual fund, or open-end investment company, must state in its prospectus whether it intends to engage in the following practices and how big a part these activities will play in their investment portfolio: buying stocks and bonds on margin, short selling, taking part in joint investment accounts, or distributing its own securities without an underwriter. If these activities aren't listed in the prospectus, in detail, the investment company is forbidden from participating in them.
- Since money market funds are not insured by the FDIC, the SEC requires that the front cover of a money market prospectus plainly state that federal government does not guarantee the money, and that there is no guarantee that the fund will be able to maintain a net asset value of one dollar. Another restriction on money market funds is that they must stay mainly invested in short-term securities—the average maturity in their portfolio cannot exceed 90 days, and no security in the portfolio can have a maturity of more than 13 months.
- Additionally, customers with cash brokerage accounts are not permitted to sell securities before they have fully paid for the shares. Doing so subjects one's account to trading restrictions for ninety days.

Closing an Account

If someone wishes to close his brokerage account, whether due to dissatisfaction with his broker, or due to a need for the funds for some other purpose, he can contract his broker with his account information and let him know. He should let his broker know if he wants any of his investment holdings to be sold or transferred to a different broker.

- If the account is not closed within three business days of the request, he should notify his broker. Regulations require that the closing of a brokerage account not be delayed except for just cause.
- After the account closure, he should check his account for any remaining funds or securities that should not have been left there.

Anti-Money Laundering (AML) Reviews

Money Laundering

Money laundering is a process by which money received illegally is given legitimacy through a legal paper trail. It is called money laundering because illegally obtained funds (dirty money) are given a legal or "clean" appearance (laundered). The Bank

Secrecy Act (BSA) requires that all broker/dealers develop anti-money laundering programs to help combat the crime.

There are three fundamental steps that criminals follow. The first step is placement in the monetary system. This is when it is easiest to catch money laundering. The next step in the money laundering process is layering. In this step, the launderers are attempting to obscure the source of the funds by transacting multiple times. These transactions can vary in many ways and help the criminal throw off investigators by varying the amounts and frequency so that they do not coincide with the crimes. Integration is the last step of money laundering. The illegal funds are intermingled with legitimate money, often by associating the illegal funds with legal funds of an actual business. This often makes the laundered funds undistinguishable from legitimate money.

Customer Screening

The Customer Identification Program (CIP) was implemented in various companies as a result of the Patriot Act, requiring financial institutions to better assess persons who wish to engage in financial activity. Each institution must employ its own CIP as befits its size and ordinary operations. CIP programs seek to assess the riskiness of their customers and verify their identities.

Know Your Customer (KYC) forms are documents specifically designed to acquire relevant information about customers, so that brokers or other agents can assess the client's willingness to assume risk, his knowledge of investments and finance, and his actual assets.

Important information about the client includes his place of residence and citizenship. Brokers should seek to gain this kind of information from their clients, such as whether they qualify as bona fide foreign residents.

Customer Information Program

The USA PATRIOT Act was initiated to help the government and financial institutions identify potential terrorist funding operations. The Customer Information Program (CIP) was established to aid financial institutions in gathering the required information. To comply with CIP, the institution must obtain the client's name, date of birth, physical address, and social security number. The CIP program is integral to the "know your customer" (KYC) controls. To meet KYC standards, the institution should start with gathering CIP information, run the client's name against lists of currently sought after parties, determine the risk associated with the customer and potential money laundering and other illegal activities, establish a normal pattern of behavior for the customer, and monitor their transactions to ensure that their behavior does not deviate from their normal patterns.

Relevance of Corporate Insiders, Employees of a Broker-Dealer, and Employees of an SRO

Corporate insiders are individuals who are particularly privy to a corporation's "inside" information; this definition includes directors and officers for the company in addition to anyone owning over 10% of the voting shares, and really anyone who has access to material but non-public knowledge. These insiders have an extra set of restrictions for any securities transactions they wish to make, and brokers should consider them accordingly.

- Another consideration which brokers have to make is whether their clients are employees of a broker-dealer. Just as corporate insiders are subject to various trading restrictions based upon their inside knowledge, so also employees of broker-dealers (especially of competing broker-dealers) carry their own set of risks. Particularly, the broker's company must receive consent from the employee's own institution.
- Employees of self-regulatory organizations (SROs) likewise are subject to these restrictions. As with employees of other broker-dealers, brokers are required to obtain the consent of a client's institution if he is employed for an SRO.

Suspicious Activity Reports

Suspicious Activities Reports (SARs) are the method by which a financial institution reports suspicious activities to the Financial Crimes Enforcement Network, or FinCEN. FinCEN is the organization that is responsible for investigating financial crimes. -Financial institutions are required to report activities that are suspicious. Such activities included transactions that are out of the norm for a client's account, transactions of cash that fall just short of reporting requirements (called structuring), transactions that derive their funding from illegal activities, transactions with no apparent purpose, transactions that facilitate suspicious or criminal activity, etc. Firms are required to file SARs in 30 days or less after becoming cognizant to the fact that suspicious transactions are occurring. SARs and related information must be maintained for 5 years. Parties that are reported in SARs must not be notified, and all information contained in the SAR is considered confidential.

OFAC

OFAC stands for the Office of Foreign Assets Control. OFAC was set up to administer and enforce economic sanctions against countries that the United States considers a threat to its national security, or that have goals that run counter to its foreign policy. The Specially Designated Nationals (SDN) list was established by OFAC for a number of reasons, among which was to assist financial institutions in preventing doing business with terrorists and other people of interest to the national security of the United States. The SDN is a list of organizations and persons that the United States bans from transacting business within its borders. Financial institutions are required to run the names of potential customers against the SDN to ensure that they are not doing business with and potentially abetting terrorists and terrorist activities.

Procedures and Reporting Related to Anti-Money Laundering Compliance

Money laundering is the deliberate concealment of the source of illegally-obtained funds, and due to its deception and harm, a number of regulations and procedures exist for anti-money laundering compliance.

- Suspicious activity reports (SARs) are made by financial institutions to the US Treasury Department (specifically, the Financial Crimes Enforcement Network, or FinCEN), detailing information about suspicious individuals or transactions.
- The Bank Secrecy Act (BSA), passed in 1970, established responsibilities for financial institutions to federal government agencies, requiring the institutions to maintain records for cash purchases of negotiable instruments, to file any such purchases totaling over $10,000, and to report any suspicious activity.
- Currency transaction reports (CTRs) must be filed by financial institutions to the federal government for any currency transaction exceeding $10,000. Before 1986, out of regard for financial privacy, these were not required.
- The Office of Foreign Asset Control (OFAC) is a section of the US Treasury Department tasked with the objective of national security other foreign policy goals through economic and trade sanctions, as well as the tracking of terrorist activity. Their relevance to anti-money laundering compliance is to discover any financial activity involving the financing of terrorism.
- The OFAC has compiled a list of Specially Designated Nationals (SDNs), that is, people or groups of people with whom US citizens and institutions are prohibited from doing business.

Maintenance of Accounts

Maintenance of Customer Account Records

Brokers have obligations not only to acquire customer information, but also to maintain their customer account records. This includes an appropriate assessment of the customer's changing assets and his investment objectives, as well as any updates for changes in address. Further, brokers must hold customer mail and send required notifications to their customers, such as the notifications required to inform customers of the risks of various accounts.

Actions That Must Be Taken After the Death of a Client

When a company is informed of the death of a client, they must immediately cancel all unfilled orders, note the accounts as "deceased," and freeze all assets until proper legal instructions are received. The executor of the deceased's estate must provide some variation of the following (contingent upon the type of account that is being settled): an official copy of the deceased party's death certificate (if applicable), any inheritance tax waivers (if applicable), and the deceased's last will and testament (if applicable).

The rules pertaining to joint accounts with rights of survivorship require that the firm be provided with an official copy of the death certificate before the deceased's interest in the account may be transferred to the other owner. Rules pertaining to accounts that are registered as joint tenants in common state that the deceased's interest are to go to their estate after the executor of the estate provides the proper documentation.

Accurate Customer Information

Firms must contact clients at least every three years to ensure that their data is up to date and complete. Should the client request a change in records regarding their investment objectives, name, address, etc., the firm must provide the customer with a copy of the changes within thirty days of receipt of notice of change.

There are many reasons why current client information is important. It provides the best service possible for the client. By ensuring you have proper client data, confirmations, statements, and other critical data are not compromised, and are received in a timely fashion. Firms should also keep current records to ensure that they are in compliance with the Customer Information Program, and are doing their best to prevent fraudulent financial activities.

Reasons an Account Might Be Restricted or Frozen

When an account is frozen, all open orders must be canceled. No further transactions may take place in the account. No money may be withdrawn from or deposited to the account. The assets may not be moved to another account. No action at all may be taken with the account. This usually occurs when an account has been identified as potentially aiding terrorist or drug activity. Freezing may also occur when the owner of the account has died. This is to prevent fraudulent activity from occurring in the owners account. These accounts are especially easy targets, as there is no one to report suspicious activity.

There are different levels of restricted accounts. The most common type of restriction is a trading restriction on the account. In this case, cash may still be withdrawn and usually assets may be transferred, but transactions may not occur in the account. This is usually due to improper documentation on file. Once the documentation is resolved, the restriction is removed.

Special Considerations for Accounts of Associated Persons of Member Firms

As employees of firms associated with the Financial Industry Regulatory Authority (FINRA), representatives often receive benefits such as discounted trading fees when they use their employing firm to hold their assets. Situations such as these do not call for additional record keeping. However if an employee of a FINRA firm holds an account with another FINRA member, many times the employing firm will charge the employee to keep track of both accounts. Additionally, the firm where the assets are held is required to provide duplicate statements to the employing firm. They are only required to so, however, when the employing firm requests it. The right to request the duplicate statements of the account is the exclusive right of the employing firm. Other FINRA members may not make similar requests.

Types of Disclosures

Illiquid Securities

Illiquid securities are those securities for which there are not a high enough demand to buy and/or sell them on demand, or securities that require a long turnaround time. The most common examples of illiquid assets are real estate, penny stocks (stocks that trade for less than $5 and are not listed on major exchanges), and non-publicly traded securities.

Real estate, even if there is high demand for it, may take an extended period of time to close a sale. Large amounts of penny stocks can be difficult to sell, as there may not be a high demand for them. Securities that are not publicly traded can also be difficult to sell as they are not listed on major exchanges; they also carry more risk because they were not registered with the Securities Exchange Commission (SEC) as publicly traded stocks are. Customers should be made aware of these risks, and their goals and tolerances should be examined to ensure that an illiquid investment will not inhibit their ability to meet daily necessities.

Accounts That Require Disclosure

There are two types of accounts that require additional disclosure regarding risk to clients. Options accounts require that the options disclosure document (ODD) be given to the client. Options carry different levels of risk, dependent upon the type of option. While covered calls only carry the risk of having to sell a security that one owns, uncovered calls come with unlimited risk. The risk varies dependent upon the option. The client must be made aware of the inherent riskiness of the options so that they do not suffer large unexpected losses that they may not be able to make up before they need access to the money.

Margin accounts are accounts wherein the client may borrow money from the brokerage to buy securities. Margin accounts ultimately magnify the result of investment. A large loss (or gain) may be turned into a much larger loss (or gain) due to nature of buy and selling with borrowed funds. Clients must be aware that there is potential for larger than normal losses, and interest may be owed on monies borrowed.

Margin Accounts and Day Trading Accounts

Margin trading can be profitable, but it includes risks of loss greater than with buying stocks with cash, and customers wishing to trade on margin must be informed of these risks. This notification must be provided by the broker before the client opens a margin account, and the client must be reminded of the risks every year, in writing. You must let customers know that because since they're using borrowed money, it is quite possible that they'll lose more money than they have in their account. You must also tell them that margin calls must be met immediately, that borrowing rules are subject to change at any time, and that if some of their stocks must be sold to meet a margin call, the brokerage house and not the customer chooses which stocks will be sold.

Some brokerage firms actively encourage day trading and specialize in catering to day trading clients. These firms have a special obligation to educate their customers who are potential day traders in order to make sure they have some idea of what day trading entails and the risks involved. They must furnish to the customer a risk disclosure form which outlines all the risks involved in day trading, and they must specifically approve the account for day trading, or have the client sign a form affirming that they don't intend to use the account to day trade.

Due to the increased risks of margin accounts, brokerage firms must disclose some of the risks to customers. For instance, customers should know that they can lose more funds than they deposit, that they might be forced to sell assets in their accounts (or that the brokerage firm might itself sell such assets), and that the brokerage firm's maintenance margin requirement might increase. Since the broker is lending money to the client, it is imperative that the broker or firm disclose the rate of interest the client will be charged for the borrowed money. Likewise, since the client will have to collateralize some assets in order to hold the account, the broker should disclose information to the client regarding such hypothecation.

Offering Documents, Prospectuses, and Red Herrings

Offering documents are disclosures provided by issuers of securities providing specific and detailed financial information concerning both the issuer and the offering itself.

Prospectuses are formal documents which brokers are legally required to file with the SEC. They provide information about investments being offered for sale to the public, giving information so that investors can make intelligent and informed decisions. Stocks and bonds have two types of prospectuses, preliminary and final.

Red herrings are preliminary prospectuses. They are called such, not because they are misleading (as are "red herrings" in logic and rhetoric), but because they include a statement in red lettering on the cover declaring that they are preliminary, and thus that some items might be subject to change.

Statements of Additional Information, Material Events, and Control Relationships

Statements of additional information, sometimes abbreviated as SAIs, are supplementary documents which are added to prospectuses for mutual fund offerings. These statements provide further details on the fund, although they are not strictly necessary for investors to make informed decisions, and therefore they are not legally required by fund companies to include. (However, they must provide such information for free to customers upon request.)

Material events are any events which substantively impact a prospective investor's decision to invest or not. These can be economic events, political events, or anything else. Brokers should be aware of these and report them to customers as is appropriate.

In order to avoid conflicts of interest and thereby protect customers, brokers are required to disclose any control relationships they have with the issuer of securities, bonds in particular. Although the initial disclosure can be merely verbal, before a transaction actually goes through, the customer must be informed in writing of the control issue. This usually takes place at confirmation.

Basic Disclosure Required for Municipal Fund Securities Advertisements

According to the MSRB, product advertisements for municipal fund securities must include a basic disclosure which states (a) that investors should carefully consider the costs and risks of such securities, (b) that further information on municipal fund securities is available in the issuer's official statement, (c) that the broker is the underwriter of the securities for which the official statement (mentioned elsewhere in the advertisement) can be supplied, if he indeed is, and (d) that the official statement should be carefully read.

Options Disclosure Document (ODD)

Options are riskier than other types of investments, so before engaging in their first options transaction, investors are required to receive an Options Disclosure Document (ODD) that articulates these increased risks and their tax implications. (For instance, if the investor is selling call options, he could have an unlimited maximum loss potential.) The investor must read and sign this document before his brokerage account is permitted to include options.

Additional Disclosures Required for Municipal Fund Securities Advertisements

Municipal securities advertisements are also required to offer a legend explaining the relevance of performance data, noting that future results cannot be guaranteed on the basis of past performance, that an investor may lose more than his original investment, and that even current performance may be worse than the (past) performance indicated in the advertisement.

Additionally, such advertisements should note any sales loads or other nonrecurring fee, including whether such fees are reflected in the advertisement's performance data.

Lastly, to whatever extent this is applicable to the performance data, the advertisement should include the total annual operating expense ratio of municipal securities (gross of fee waivers or expense reimbursements).

Day Trading Risk Disclosure Statement

Day Trading Risk Disclosure Statement (FINRA Rule 2270) - in addition to providing the customer with the risk disclosure statement, the member must post the same disclosure on the member's website. The risks disclosures include: day trading is extremely risky; be cautious of claims of large profits from day trading; day trading requires knowledge of securities markets; day trading requires knowledge of a firm's operations; day trading will generate substantial commissions, even if the per trade cost is low; day trading on margin or short selling may result in losses beyond your initial investment; and potential registration requirements.

Basic Knowledge of Cashiering and Account Transfers

Movement of Funds and Securities

Transferring Funds

There are three methods by which money may be moved to, from, and between accounts. They are wire transfers, movement by automated clearing house (ACH), and movement by check. Wire transfers transfer funds to or from accounts are electronic transactions that move money between bank accounts. The accounts between which the money is transferred may be in the same registration, or between different parties. Another form of electronic transfer is an ACH payment. Automated clearing house transactions are large batches of electronic transactions that are disseminated between financial institutions. ACH payments are a part of a large batch, while wires are for single transactions. Money may also be moved between accounts in the more traditional form of a paper check. A check is a paper negotiable instrument whereby account owners may transport large sums of money between accounts.

Letters of Authorization

Since the custodian of a new account is not actually the owner of the account, they may not request the funds from the customer's old account. The customer then must provide a letter of authorization to the old custodian to transfer custodianship to the new custodian. The letter that the customer sends should contain account details such as the account number, how much of the account that should be transferred, how the transfer should be executed, and the customer's name.

Moving the account via ACATS usually includes the firm that is receiving the funds submitting an "ACAT form" that includes the customers' name, Social Security number, the registration of the account to be moved, the type and amount assets to be moved, and the customer's signature. If any of these requirements are abnormal, the firm currently holding the assets may reject the form.

Medallion Signature Guarantee Program

The Medallion Signature Guarantee Program was developed by the New York Stock Exchange to provide a service whereby signatures may be guaranteed and endorsed by a reputable firm. One of the most common uses of the Medallion Signature Guarantee Program is for transfer agents to ensure that signatures on certificates that are required to be guaranteed are accepted. To participate in the program (participants are usually banks and FINRA firms), an annual fee and administrative expenses must be paid. While the Medallion Signature stamp guarantees the signature, it does not guarantee the document. The types of documents that the program covers are securities (i.e., physical stock certificates), stock and bond powers (powers to transact physical stock certificates), certificates of deposit, land deeds, and other documents that are subject to fraudulent activity.

Currency Transaction Reporting

To help combat money laundering, any time a deposit of over $10,000 in cash in one day is made to a financial institution, the depositor must file a Currency Transaction Report. This is a requirement of the Bank Secrecy Act. CTRs are filed on Form 104. Form 104 must be completed with the customer's personal information (including method of verifying the customer's identity), the type and amount of transaction, and the financial institution's information. All records pertaining to Form 104 must be held for at least five years. If a CTR is not filed, the financial institution is subject to a fine of up to $500,000 and/or the responsible individual could face 10 years in federal prison. The CTR must be filed within fifteen days of the occurrence of a qualifying event.

Reinvesting and Sweeping the Cash That an Investment Generates

When an investment provides some return other than capital appreciation, such as interest from certificates of deposit or dividends from stocks or mutual funds, that money must be held in an appropriate account. If a client chooses to reinvest the dividends, they receive additional shares of the security equivalent to the dividend paid, and the value is retained in the account. If they would rather have access to the cash, they may choose for the cash to be deposited into the account. Sweep accounts are typically set up for this arrangement because they provide the investor with additional protection. Since broker/dealers are member of the SIPC and not the FDIC, accounts are established for the client at an FDIC member bank and the cash is "swept" to that account to receive the additional protection of the FDIC. While the client's funds at the broker/dealer are covered up to the maximum, they also benefit from their cash being covered at the FDIC. This is most helpful when they exceed the maximum SIPC protection.

Transfer or Partial Transfers of Accounts Between Broker/Dealers

Automated Customer Account Transfer Service (ACATS)

The Automated Customer Account Transfer Service allows broker/dealers to transfer funds and securities to other broker/dealers electronically. The receiving firm will provide an ACAT form to the sending firm that requests the funds and/or securities. The holding firm must respond to the request in one business day after they receive the request. They must fulfill the request unless the account does not contain transferable assets, the customer's social is incorrect, the registration of the account requested does not match their records, or there is no signature (or an irregular customer signature) on the form. If the form is rejected, action must be taken by the applicable firm within 5 business days. After the holding firm approves the form, they must freeze the account and cancel all orders excluding options. The holding firm then has three days to transfer the account to the receiving firm. ACATS transfers are not exclusive to full transfers; partial account transfers may be accomplished with ACATS.

Internal Transfers, Such as Transfer on Death (TOD), and Divorce

Internal transfers are transfers which customers make with funds between or among their own accounts (or accounts with which they are closely associated).

Transfer on death (TOD) permits securities to pass from an account owner directly to some assigned TOD beneficiary upon the owner's death. The benefit of this is that such a transfer eliminates the need to go through probate. In this type of transfer, however, the beneficiaries need to ensure that the transferred funds and assets are re-registered in their own names.

Divorce transfers can vary according to the terms specified by the parties to be divorced. It is not uncommon for brokerage accounts to be split 50-50.

Residual Credits

Residual credits are credits to an account that are deposited to the account after an account has been transferred to another financial institution. Residual credits usually deposit to an investment account in the form of a dividend from a stock, mutual fund, investment trust, etc., that is paid after the account is transferred. These credits can be in the form of cash or securities, dependent upon whether the customer has elected to receive the dividends in cash form or in the form of additional securities (referred to as reinvestment of dividends). After the holding firm that delivered the account to the receiving firm identifies these residual credits, they must transfer these assets as well. This process does not require an additional ACAT form or letter of authorization, as the credit is a by-product of the securities already transferred.

Handling Checks

Negotiable Checks

Negotiable checks, sometimes referred to as negotiable instruments, are paper documents that allow the transport of large amounts of funds with a single negotiation. To be negotiable, the check must have a valid date, a payee, a legal written amount, and the signature of the account owner. To negotiate the check, the payee must endorse (sign) the back of the check. In this manner, the check may be made payable to a third party. The original payee must endorse the check and write "pay to the order of" and the new payee's name to make it payable to a third party. Some financial institutions will not honor checks with third party payees, as they are more susceptible to fraudulent activities. Additionally, unless the check is being deposited to the payee's account, most financial institutions will require some type of verification of the customer's identity before they negotiate the instrument.

Issuing a Check to Ensure That It Is Accepted for Payment by a Broker/Dealer

Since most broker/dealers do not accept, hold, or distribute cash, sometimes issuing a check is the most convenient way to contribute to an investment account. If a check is improperly issued, the broker/dealer will reject the check to prevent the paying bank from denying funds to the broker/dealer.

To be sure that the check is acceptable to the broker/dealer, several qualifications must be met. The check may not be stale-dated, or dated with a date greater than six months prior to the date of presentation. The check must also be made payable to the proper person. A check made payable to an individual may not be deposited to a joint account of which that individual is a co-owner; it should be made payable to both parties. Acceptance of third-party checks is at the discretion of the receiving financial institution.

Check Blotters

Broker/dealers are required by federal law to maintain a daily record of all checks that are deposited with the firm. The blotter should be updated at least daily with a description of all checks that they receive. The information about the check that should be collected and recorded is the date on which the checks were received, the person who remitted the check, and the monetary amount of the check. Additionally, if the check is sent to another party, the blotter should contain to whom the checks were forward and on what day they were forwarded. Other more detailed information about the check is not required, but is helpful for future inquiries about the check.

Prohibited Activities Related to Cashiering and Account Transfers

Preventing Money Laundering During the Cashiering Process

The money laundering process often begins in the cashiering phase. It is especially important for the firm to note activities that may be an indication of structuring. Such activities may include making several cash deposits that aggregate just under $10,000 at different branches of the same firm. This is indicative that the potential money launderer is aware of Currency Transaction Reporting and is trying to avoid having to file Form 104. This would also be considered suspicious activity. The cashiering process is also a convenient step for the criminal to layer their ill-gotten gains. Multiple small investments in various investments can begin to give a sense of legitimacy to the funds. This may also be a convenient time for the launderer to integrate the funds with legitimate legal funds that they may have invested.

Check Fraud

Check fraud is a felony crime in the United States and will immediately disqualify a person from being registered with FINRA.

Criminals may endeavor to alter checks by changing the payee or amount, or both. The check may be legitimately made to the criminal, but they may find a way to alter the amount. The criminal may also take a legitimate check that is made payable to another party and alter the payee line so that they receive the funds.

Check kiting describes a process by which a person writes a check from one institution to another, and they do not have sufficient funds in the existing account. To cover the check, they'll write a check from another account (or the receiving account) that does not have sufficient funds. Often, check kiters do this without criminal intent, but out of desperation when they are in a financial straight. This, however, is still an illegal act, regardless of intent.

Holding Checks and Account Transfers for Extended Periods

Since checks are negotiable instruments, they are intended to be negotiated soon after issuance. Customers should not write (and financial institutions should not accept) postdated checks to be held until a later date. The customer should write the check on the day intended, and the institution should execute accordingly.

Checks should be remitted for payment promptly; this usually means within a day of receipt. However, it is acceptable to hold a check for an extended period in the event of natural disaster or national emergency that makes it impossible to determine the location and whether the funds are valid. In this case, the extenuating circumstance must be given to the Financial Industry Regulatory Authority (FINRA) in writing.

Likewise, a broker/dealer should not hold a valid request to transfer an account or funds/securities. Laws state the broker/dealers should coordinate with each other and expedite their proceeds to facilitate prompt transfers of account.

Basic Knowledge of Custody and Control of Securities

Custody and Control of Securities

Safekeeping of Securities and the Segregation of Securities

Broker/dealers are obligated to ensure that their customers' funds and securities are held in a secure fashion. This includes all securities over which the firm has custody or control, without exception. Segregation describes the process of separating the firm's securities from their customers' securities. Occasionally, a customer will request that a security be registered "in street name" meaning that the security is registered to the broker/dealer but in fact belongs to the customer. Securities held in street name and securities that belong to the broker/dealer must be segregated from securities that are registered to the customer. Margined securities, however, that are used to collateralize margin accounts do not have to be segregated from broker/dealer securities.

Securities of Which a Firm Has Custody and Securities over Which the Firm Has Control

When a carrying firm is said to have custody or possession of funds and/or securities, those funds and/or securities are held "in-house" at the firm. Custodied funds have been completely purchased by the customer, and they do not owe the firm any more money for them. Funds/securities over which a broker/dealer has transactional authority but does not hold them are considered controlled funds, as the broker/dealer exerts control over the account on the customer's behalf. After the firm that custodies the funds complete all of their settlement records, there are policies and procedures in place to guarantee that the firm has taken physical custody or control over all of their customers' securities.

Securities Held in Street Name

There are several registrations under which securities may be registered. When securities are registered in street name, it means that the purchasing customer has ownership of the securities, but they are registered to the holding firm. Even though the ownership shows that the broker/dealer owns it, the customer is the actual owner and may direct the broker/dealer to transact concerning the securities.

Customers request registration in street name for convenience's sake. The broker/dealer may transact more efficiently if the securities are registered to them, and they are easier for the firm to provide safekeeping.

Directly Held Mutual Funds

Directly held mutual funds are mutual funds that are owned by an individual, partnership, or corporation and are held in beneficial ownership for the owner at the investment company that issues the mutual fund. Broker/dealers do not service directly held mutual funds, although the investment company may allow them informational access to mutual client's holdings for the client's convenience, but only at the client's request. Any transactions executed pertaining to the directly held funds must be requested at the mutual fund.

Directly held mutual funds typically offer lower account fees than full brokerage accounts. This assists smaller investors with less complex needs. Directly held mutual fund accounts, however, are much less flexible than brokerage accounts. Multiple types of investments and products from multiple investment companies may be held in a brokerage account, whereas a directly held mutual fund account will only hold mutual funds that are issued by that investment company.

Keeping a Customer's Funds in a Safe Location

For a broker/dealer to take possession of a client's funds, they must have an agreement with a firm that can guarantee the safekeeping of those funds. Firms that offer and meet those standards of safekeeping are firms such as commercial banks, other broker/dealers that offer to hold them, and depository trust companies. Some foreign banks, clearing houses, and depositories qualify for this distinction, but only if they have approved by the Securities Exchange Commission (SEC).

Depository trust companies can hold nearly any security. This makes them a very convenient repository for firms that have clients with needs that require access to and the ability to hold more than one type of security. Depository trust companies may not hold securities that are subject to certain types of restrictions such as ownership restrictions. Given their flexibility concerning security types, depository trust companies are the largest holder of securities in the world.

Process Required for Carrying Firms to Perform a Periodic Physical Count of the Securities They Hold

According to SEC rule 17a-13, all firms that hold securities must perform a physical inventory check each quarter, sometimes called a box count. The count must be a performed by a person other than one whose regular job is the care and custody of the funds and securities held at that firm. This is to prevent fraud by someone who has the means to conceal the fraud for a long period of time. The person who performs the count must count each security of which the firm has possession, and all securities of which they will soon have custody and control such as those in transit to the firm at a transfer agency. They must also provide for those securities over which the firm would have had control, but have not received because of failures to deliver or receive.

In the event that the quarterly physical count of the firm's holdings does not match the records that the firm keeps in the stock record, action must be taken to rectify the difference. If the count reveals more securities than the stock record shows, they are said to have a long securities difference. If the count reveals fewer securities, they are said to have a short securities difference.

In the case of a long securities difference, the firm may sell the excess securities to balance the count, but they must charge the amount of the sale against their net worth. They may also only hold the securities without affecting their net worth. It is the position of the Securities Exchange Commission that the firm will eventually determine the actual owner. In this event, if the securities were sold, the customer must be made whole. In the event of a short difference, the firm must make up the difference if the securities are not located within 45 days.

SECURITIES TRANSFERS

REGISTERED CERTIFICATES AND BEARER CERTIFICATES

Bonds were once issued to investors as bearer bonds, or bearer certificates. Bearer bonds were not registered to the investor. These bonds had physical coupons attached to them. Anyone who had possession of the coupon could redeem the coupon. The investor would clip the coupon and remit the coupon to issuer's paying firm, and the firm would pay the investor the amount of the coupon. This is from where the term coupon payment comes when referring to the interest payment of a registered bond. There are still assumed to be some bearer bonds in existence, but they are no longer issued. Registered bonds are registered to an investor. The interest payment is paid only to the registered investor, usually in the form of a deposit to the investor's brokerage account. They are much more secure and convenient to investors than bearer bonds.

GOOD DELIVERY AND TRANSFER AGENTS

Good delivery describes securities that have been delivered in good order with all requirements present that are necessary for transfer. Such requirements are the signature required to transfer the security to another ownership, the denomination must be in the appropriate amount, the physical condition of the certificate (if it is a physical certificate) must be acceptable, and any applicable attachments must be present. Good delivery usually only applies to transactions between dealers, but occasionally a customer will be required to provide good delivery to a dealer if they have made a sell to the dealer that requires good delivery. The transfer agent is the party that determines if a delivery of securities is good or not. Transfer agents review the delivery ticket and securities delivered to ensure that all of the good delivery requirements are met.

Good delivery involves the requirements that must be met for a security in a transaction to be transferred to a buyer. A security certificate meeting these requirements is ready to be transferred "on good delivery." Otherwise, the trade cannot be settled.

Some of the general requirements for good delivery are that the certificate must be in good physical condition (i.e. not mutilated), that the certificate must have an endorsement, that the exact number of securities (whether shares or bonds) must be delivered, and that the correct currency denomination for the certificates must be delivered.

Good Delivery Requirements for Bonds

Bearer bonds (a.k.a. coupon bonds), which are not registered to particular individuals, but are as tradeable and liquid as dollar bills, must be delivered with all the related unpaid coupons—the interest payments—attached to them in order to be in good form.

Registered bonds, which *are* registered to particular individuals, must have par values in multiples of $1,000, not to exceed $100,000, in order to be delivered in good form.

Good Delivery Requirements for Stock

To be delivered in good form, stock certificates are required to be denominated in ways relating to a *round lot*, that is, 100 shares. The certificates must be denominated in multiples of 100 shares (100, 200, 300, etc.), divisors of 100 shares (100, 50, 25, 20, 10, 5, etc.), or units adding up to 100 shares (30+70, 37+59+4, etc.).

- Trades of fewer than 100 shares are termed *odd lot trades*, and discrete components of trades which are fewer than 100 shares can be termed *odd lot portions*. These are not required to meet this particular good delivery requirement.
- For example, in a trade of 430 shares, if the trade were comprised of two 200-share certificates and a 30-share certificate, the trade would be in good delivery form, since the two 200-share certificates would be multiples of 100, and since the 30-share certificate would be exempt as an odd lot portion. However, if the trade were comprised of one 300-share certificate and two 65-share certificates, then it would not be in good form, since, while the 300-share certificate is valid as a multiple of 100 shares, the two 65-share certificates do not meet any of the requirements and are not exempt as an odd lot portion.

Endorsements, Transfer Agents, and Registrars

Endorsements refer to the signing of some document which effectively permits for some money or asset to be transferred to a different person.

A transfer agent is a person or institution that acts on behalf of a corporation to keep track of investors and their activities, including account balances and account transactions. Transfer agents also help with the mailing and canceling of stock certificates, and deals with any problems investors may have, such as lost stock certificates.

Whenever transfer agents facilitate the transfer of a stock from one shareholder to another, there are specific *transfer procedures* which they must follow, as outlined by the SEC.

Registrars are similar to transfer agents, working with them to keep track of stockholders and bondholders. The primary objective for registrars is to ensure that the number of outstanding shares do not surpass the quantity of authorized stock for the company.

Stock and Bond Powers and Their Role in the Validation of Securities

Stock and bond powers are certain authorities granted to a party to transact a given stock or bond on behalf of another party. For a security to be validated, the owner must endorse (usually by signing) the certificate. A stock or bond power may be submitted with a security certificate in lieu of endorsing the security. This is a more secure way for the client to transact, since an endorsed security may be registered to anyone. The client may sign a stock or bond power for their broker/dealer to transact a physical certificate for them, thus reducing the risk of loss and theft. A single stock or bond power may provide for the transaction of multiples of the same security, but each separate security requires a new stock or bond power.

Direct Registration System and Deposit/Withdrawal at Custodian

The Direct Registration System (DRS) and Deposit/Withdrawal at Custodian (DWAC) are methods of transferring a customer's securities electronically. The Direct Registration System allows the customer to transfer securities that are registered in the customer's name between the transfer agent and the firm that is receiving the securities by means of electronic systems. It should be noted that the securities must be registered to the customer for this method; registration in street name is not accept from transfer via the Direct Registration System. Deposit/Withdrawal at Custodian differs from DRS in that the entire process is not accomplished electronically. The customer must provide a medallion signature guaranteed stock power to facilitate the transfer.

Depository Eligible Securities

The most common types of securities that are depository eligible are stocks, warrants, rights, corporate bonds and notes, municipal bonds, closed-end fund shares (i.e., exchange traded funds), depositary receipts, money market instruments, and government securities. While these are the most common types of depositable securities, they are not exclusively depository eligible.

The basic requirements for a security to be depository eligible are that it must be registered according to the Securities Act of 1933 or be obtained in a transaction exempting the security from registration according to the Securities Act of 1933 with no ownership restrictions, and be resalable under Rule 144A or Regulation S of the Securities Act of 1933. Rule 144 dictates the treatment of securities that are deemed to be controlled or restricted securities.

Stock Legends

Stock legends are special qualifications that are printed on a stock certificate. For the certificate to be negotiable, the legend on the stock must be fulfilled. Stock legends are typically placed on stocks that are restricted because they have not been registered with the Securities Exchange Commission (SEC). These restrictive legends are most commonly found on stock certificates of privately held companies. The language of most stock legends explains the restrictions of transfer to the holder. Other than legends restricting unregistered securities, some privately held companies place legends on their company's stock certificates to control who may or may not become a shareholder.

Securities Exchange Commission's Rule 144

The Securities Exchange Commission's Rule 144 sets forth legal processes for dealing with control and restricted securities. Persons with control stock of a company are those persons who are officers, directors, affiliated persons, or persons owning 10% or greater of the company's stock. Individuals with control securities are limited as the number of securities that are allowed to sell within a given time period. This limitation is in place for as long as they are a control person. There is no holding period for control securities, unless they are unregistered.

Under Rule 144, restricted stocks are defined as securities that are acquired via a private placement, or any other method of obtaining a stock that has not been registered. The investor must hold the stock (after it has been fully paid) for at least 6 months before they may begin selling shares, and then the selling is subject to a volume limit, as in the case of control securities.

Basic Knowledge of Trade Reporting and Trade Corrections

Automated Confirmation Transaction Service

The Automated Confirmation Transaction (ACT) Service is an electronic system for tracking and reporting trades. The ACT Service is jointly operated and administered by FINRA and NASDAQ. ACT reports trades to the National Securities Clearing Corporation (to facilitate settlement and clearing) on behalf of those firms that use ACT. It is important to note that ACT is not a method of order entry; all orders that are reported via ACT have already been confirmed. Thus, all trades that are reported through ACT are considered "locked in" and are sent to the National Securities Clearing Corporation and must be settled according to the regular settlement schedule. ACT users may report up to 500 trades at in time.

Trade Reporting and Compliance Engine

The Trade Reporting and Compliance Engine, or TRACE, is an electronic reporting system used by FINRA to report the trading of debt securities that are placed "Over-the-Counter," or OTC. TRACE is not an order-entry method; it is used as automatically report trading. The information reported through TRACE is made available to the public as a means of promoting market transparency. The information reported through TRACE is the time and date of execution, the price at execution, the number of securities traded, the yield of the instrument, whether the trade was reported promptly, whether the price includes the commission charged, and whether there was a unique condition or settlement that affected the price. Not all debt securities are eligible to be reported via TRACE. Such securities include foreign debt, the United States Treasury, money markets, physical debt securities, convertible bonds, primary offerings, agency debentures, and municipal securities.

Trade Reporting and Comparison Service

The Trade Reporting and Comparison Service (TRACS) was developed for those firms that are not eligible to use the Automated Confirmation Transaction Service (ACT). This is usually because they are not members of the NASDAQ, rather they are an alternative display facility (ADF). TRACS facilitates the requirement that trades be reported within 30 seconds of execution. TRACS, unlike ACT, will allow the reporting firm to report three-party trades. TRACS has much in common with ACT, including the reporting of locked-in trades and providing a comparison service to view other trades that are public information. Like ACT, TRACS is not an order-entry system, but a reporting and comparison system. If a firm is a member of the NASDAQ and an ADF, they may choose to report via either TRACS or ACT.

Strategies Associated with Only Buying and Selling Securities

Buying pertains to purchasing a security for an investment, while selling is selling an investment to another investor. There are strategies involved with each. Each may be done "at the market," or at the next available price, or they may have qualifiers attached to them that require them to be bought or sold at a certain price. The qualifiers are called stops and limits, and will trigger purchases or sells, or prevent transactions from occurring according to the investor's instructions.

The difference in selling long and selling short is that when an investor sells an asset short, they do not own it, and must borrow the security. They hope the security will decrease in value so they can buy the security at a lower price than they borrowed it at, and return the borrowed security to the lending broker. Holding a long position refers to traditional investing (buying and holding an asset in hopes of capital appreciation).

Covered and an Uncovered (Naked) Position

Uncovered, or naked, and covered positions usually refer to options positions. A naked position is one in which the investor does not own the security on which the option is based. Naked positions are much riskier than covered positions, because if the underlying asset moves in an unfavorable way, it could be untenable for the investor to cover the loss. For example, a covered call is generally considered the safest option to sell. If the value of the underlying security increases and the position is called, the customer only has to sell a security they already own. Uncovered calls, however, are generally considered the riskiest types of option. The value of the underlying security theoretically may increase infinitely, and since the investor doesn't own the security, they must buy it to meet the call, and they are at the mercy of the market as to price.

Bearish and Bullish

If an investor is said to be bearish, they believe that the market is going to decline soon, or that it is already in a state of decline. Bullish investors believe that there is a very positive outlook for the markets. Bearish investors may take steps to prepare for a bear market, such as selling positions short and selling their long positions to hold cash. Bearish investors may also buy assets that are negatively correlated to the market that they believe will decline. An investor that is bearish on equities will move funds to bonds since the two share a negative correlation. In the event that bearish investors do not want to sell their long positions, they may also use options to hedge their long positions to protect against loss.

Bullish investors tend to hold current investments hoping that they will increase. Like bearish investors, bullish investors write options, too, but with the intent of magnifying gains instead of hedging losses. Bullish investors tend not to hold cash, as they believe it can best be put to work in the market.

Best Execution

Best execution refers to a broker/dealer obtaining the most favorable situation for a customer's order. This means getting the most favorable price, filling the order with the most speed, whether the entire order is being filled, etc.

It is the obligation of the broker/dealer to ensure that the customer is receiving the best execution with each of their orders. FINRA reviews its members' records to determine whether the customers are receiving the best execution. The four most common (and most telling) areas which FINRA reviews are the availability of quotes for the security, the amount and type of transaction, how many markets the broker/dealer checked, and the trading characteristics of the market for the security, such as volume and price.

Trading Capacities in Which Agents Work for Customers or for Themselves

When a representative works in an agent capacity for a customer, they are acting as a broker. Brokers work to find other investors that either desire to buy the security that their customer wants to sell or sell the security that their customer wants to buy. When a representative acts in a broker capacity, they are usually paid a percentage of the total transaction. A broker/dealer that sells from his or her own inventory is acting in a dealer capacity. If a customer wants to buy a certain security and the dealer has it on hand, they may sell it to the customer from their stock of securities. They make money doing this by charging a markup, or an increase in the price that they paid for the security. Dealers may keep a large stock of high-volume securities on hand, both to better serve their customers with quicker executions and to benefit from the markups that they will receive.

Quotations

Quotations are the price at which a dealer will be willing to buy or sell a security. A quote is comprised of a bid price and offer price. The bid is the price at which the dealer will buy the security from a customer. The offer or ask price is the price at which the dealer will sell the security to the customer. To ensure that the dealer is paid and receives its markup, the "ask" or offer price will always be higher than the bid price. The difference in the bid and offer prices is called the spread. If a customer receives a quote as "bid 35, ask 36," they may buy the security at 36 and sell it at 35, and the spread is 1.

Market Hours

Normal market hours are measured by the hours that the New York Stock Exchange (NYSE) keeps. Normal trading hours at the NYSE are from 9:30 am to 4:00 pm Eastern Time. Over-the-counter and secondary market trading usually keep the same hours as the NYSE, but some market makers keep extended hours. Extended trading hours begin at 9:30 Eastern with the NYSE, but stay open until 6:30 pm to facilitate late buyers and sellers. Trading volume between 4:00 and 6:30 is typically much lower than normal trading hours. Because of the low volume of trading there is less liquidity in the markets; fewer people want to buy and sell. This results in larger spreads between bid and ask prices; the holders of the securities may charge more than normal because the supply drops significantly during after-hours trading, and may pay less, because there are fewer buyers.

Trader Errors

If trader places an order error, they must follow a process to correct it. Since corrections are made after the original trade date, the new order must be backdated to reflect the customer's original intent. This is known as the "as/of" property of a corrected trade. The records will show the correction trade being entered as normal, but it will be marked "as/of" to reflect the date that it should have been processed. Firms have error accounts in which they cover trader errors, but it is not an account for regular use.

The settlement date of corrected trades will use the "as/of" date to start the settlement period. Thus, if a trade has been unchanged for a day before the error is caught, the settlement time is T+0 from the revision trade instead of the normal T+1. If the error was not caught within the normal settling time, however, the trade will settle in the normal period following the revision trade.

Front Running and Excessive Trading

Front running describes the practice of employees of FINRA members placing trades in their personal account when they know that the security that they transacted is about to be block traded elsewhere. Block trading is an order consisting of 10,000 or more shares of a security. This gives the FINRA member representative an opportunity to take advantage of a significant price change, and it is considered insider knowledge. Excessive trading, sometimes called churning, describes the practice of representatives placing more trades in a customer's account than is necessary, or placing unnecessarily large trades. This is done to create extra commissions for the representative. Churning is illegal and unethical even if it creates return for the customer.

Market Manipulation

Market manipulation is the attempts by a trader or an investor to change market outcomes to suit their needs, instead of letting the markets take their normal course. Market manipulation is always illegal. The most common types of market manipulation are capping (selling large quantities of securities to keep the price down), supporting (entering buy orders to keep the price of a security up, or support it), pegging (entering buy and sell orders to keep the price from moving), front running (trading ahead of block orders to take advantage of the price movement), and spinning (sending initial public offering shares to a person who may be in a position to send more business to the firm).

Excessive Markups and Reasonable Markups

Markups are the method by which dealers are paid for securities that they sell from their inventory. Charging excessive markups is an unethical practice. Unscrupulous dealers may attempt to charge larger than normal markups to investors that are unaware of normal markups. A maximum of 5% markup is considered the high limit of normal markups.

Excessive markups are determined based upon many factors. The markup should be relatively similar to other dealers' markups, be reasonable based upon the effort it took to acquire the securities, and be reasonable based on the other services offered and expenses incurred associate with the security. These factors can occasionally lead to markups of less the 5% being considered excessive. Also, it should be noted that the 5% rule is relative to the predominant market prices; a dealer that charges a 1% markup but inflates the security price to charge a higher markup has still practiced excessive marking up.

Breakpoint Sales

While the term breakpoint describes a discount for volume in commission paid, the term breakpoint sales refers to the practice of selling a product just below the breakpoint to avoid a reduction in commission. This practice is unethical and does not constitute fair trading. It is possible for an unethical representative to obtain a higher commission on a smaller investment than they would have on a larger investment using breakpoint sales. It is critical to be aware of breakpoint limits; a breakpoint sale is still unethical even if it is unintentional. In the event that the customer is near the breakpoint, but does not have funds to meet the breakpoint, the representative should talk to the customer about a letter of intent to buy more of the product, which may result in the customer getting the breakpoint rate.

Acceptable and Unacceptable Practices of Sharing Profits and Losses in a Customer's Account

In very rare cases, some representatives share accounts with their customers. Usually, representatives are not allowed to share accounts with clients unless it is approved by a registered principal with authority over the representative, and the profits and losses are equally shared by both parties. If a representative were to take on a disproportionate share of losses, it could be a form of guaranteeing returns and strictly forbidden. Likewise, the FINRA member employees would not be allowed to accept more return than is proportionate to their participation in the account. The only exception to this rule is for the customer to be an immediate family member of the representative. Typically, registered principals find it very difficult to determine proportionality and find it inefficient to permit such accounts.

PROHIBITED ACTIVITIES FOR BROKERS

Brokers are legally prohibited from engaging in a number of behaviors designed to unduly benefit themselves or hurt others.

- They are not permitted to spread market rumors in order to influence other people to buy or sell a security. This is because market transactions ought to be based on real facts and knowledge.
- They are not permitted to engage in frontrunning, which is when a broker makes a trade due to his foreknowledge of a block trade (a trade of 10,000+ stocks) before it is reported.
- They are not permitted to engage in churning, which occurs when a broker participates in excessive trading on a client's behalf only to obtain extra commissions.
- They are not permitted to engage in commingling, which is the combination of a customer's fully-paid securities and his margined securities, or the combination of a customer's securities with a firm's securities.
- They are not permitted to prearrange trades, which would be an agreement between a broker and a customer to buy back some security at a given price.
- They are not permitted to guarantee against losses, since that would be frankly misrepresenting the riskiness of investments.
- They are not permitted to pay for referrals by compensating others (whether with cash or something else) for finding, introducing, or referring a client.
- They are not permitted to make unsuitable recommendations, which is simply to say that they ought to recommend good investments. If this is serious enough, customers can sue brokers for failing in their obligations.

Basic Knowledge of Corporate Actions

TYPES OF CORPORATE ACTIONS

ACTIONS A CORPORATION MAY TAKE IN THE EVENT THAT THEY DECIDE IT IS ADVANTAGEOUS TO ADJUST THEIR STOCK PRICE

For a corporation to intentionally and legally lower their stock price, they may split their stock. A stock split is an event in which a corporation lowers their stock price, usually to give access to a broader range of investors and issues additional stock to those affected by the split. A stock that experienced a 2:1 split at $50 per share would cause current shareholders to own twice as much stock at half the value. If the investor held 100 shares, they would now have 200 shares at $25 per share. Similarly, if a company wanted to make its shares more costly (usually to provide a sense of stability), the company may perform a reverse split, in which outstanding shares are reduced and the value of the shares is increased. A 1:2 reverse split would result in 100 shares of a $50 stock becoming 50 shares of a $100 stock. It is important to note that in both of the above situations, market capitalization does not change; total value remains the same.

Dividend Process and How to Handle the Processing of Customer Instructions

Some corporations that are publicly traded may issue cash payments (or additional stock) to their shareholders in the form of dividends. By regulation, companies that issue dividends must provide a ten-day notice to the exchange on which their stock is traded and to the general public. This day is called the declaration date. To receive the dividend, an investor must own the stock by the record date. The ex-dividend date is the date by which the owner must own the security in order to receive the dividend. It is two days before the record date, since most stocks settle 3 days after purchase. The payable date is the date on which the investor receives the dividend. It is usually two to three weeks after the record date. The customer may request that the dividend come to them in the form of cash or be reinvested, in which case they would receive additional stock in the company equal to the value of the dividend.

Stock Splits

A split is a change in the number of shares of stock outstanding.

The most common split is the *forward split*, which increases the number of shares outstanding, with a corresponding adjustment in share value. For example, in a 2-for-1 forward split (the most common type of split), a shareholder will receive two shares for every one they own, and the price of each new share will be half that of the former share price. Forward splits are done in most cases because a stock price has gotten so high that the cost of trading the stock has become prohibitive. More investors will be willing to buy the stock at a lower price. Forward splits are usually considered a sign of confidence on the part of the company, and it is not uncommon for share prices to rise after a forward split occurs.

A *reverse split* is the opposite—the number of shares outstanding is reduced in order to raise the price of each share, so a person who owned two shares before now owns one (in a 1-for-2 split). Reverse splits are usually considered negatively, and it is common for the price of a stock to drop after one takes place.

Spinoffs

A spinoff occurs when a corporation "spins off" (or splits off) one of its divisions/sections, making it a separate entity altogether and endowing it with particular facilities and assets.

When this occurs, shareholders in the original corporation also receive stock in the spinoff entity. Spinoffs can increase the value of stocks previously held in the one corporation before the spinoff, since it gives investors the option to choose whichever section of the company they think will be more profitable.

Delivery of Annual Reports and Notices of Corporate Actions by a Broker for His Customer

A broker is responsible for informing his customer of various actions taken by corporations in which the customer has some share or interest. This includes notifying the customer about annual reports for the corporation (as well as interim reports, if necessary) and notices of various corporate actions. If a corporation has split its stock, tendered new stock, established some kind of shareholder voting by proxy, announced plans to repurchase stock, or done some other action which is worthy of the customer's attention, the broker should seek to notify him.

Record Dates and Ex-Dividend Dates

Customers can purchase securities around the time when a company is declaring or paying dividends for their stockholders. To determine who will be entitled to receive the dividends depends on particular dates surrounding the transaction. The record date is the date when the corporation looks over its own records to identify its shareholders, and thus to identify the recipients of dividends. However, since the settlement date for securities transactions is generally three days after the execution date, only those securities purchased at least three days before the record date will receive dividends; otherwise they go to whoever held the securities previously. Because of this, the date which is two days before the record date is the ex-dividend date. On this date, since the security is recognized as not entitling the buyer to a dividend, the purchase price of the security is reduced by the value of the dividend.

Proxies and Proxy Voting

Proxy

In most cases, common stockholders have the right to vote on major changes (i.e., election of board members) at the annual shareholders' meeting. While common stock owners have the option of attending the meeting, it is often inconvenient for them to attend due to prior obligation, distance to the meeting, or some other extenuating circumstance. If a shareholder is unable to attend the meeting, they may appoint a proxy and give them a limited power of attorney concerning the vote. The proxy will cast the owner's vote in their place. Appointment of a proxy is usually accomplished by mail or electronically, with assistance from the customer's broker.

Manner in Which FINRA Member Firms Are Required to Assist Issuers in Disseminating Important Documents to Their Shareholders

Since many firms hold stock in street name for the convenience of their clients, the issuers of the stock do not have records of the customers to send them important documents, such as annual and interim reports. The nominal owners of the street name stock, that is the carrying firm, must ensure that the beneficial owners (customers who actually own the street name stock) get those documents. All proxy material and regular reports are sent to the carrying firm, and the carrying firm must forward those materials to the beneficial owners. The issuer in turn is obligated to reimburse any costs (such as employee hours and any postage incurred) that are associated with the delivery of the materials to the client.

Basic Knowledge of Margin and Stock Loan/Securities Lending

Margin

Investment margin is essentially a line of credit that is extended to a customer. Margin may be used in one of two ways; to purchase securities or withdraw as cash. Customers typically use margin to speculate on the movement of securities or to add liquidity to their account. They may withdraw cash from their margin balance, if the need arises, so that they do not have to liquidate positions to cover the withdrawal.

Customers who use margin to purchase securities typically do so to magnify their gains. If they have only enough cash to purchase 100 shares of XYZ and desire to purchase 200 shares, they may use margin to purchase the extra shares. If the price of XYZ increases, their gains are magnified by the amount purchased on margin (the margin must still be repaid, but they may keep the extra gains). However, if XYZ decreases, their loss is magnified; not only did they lose money on the investment, they now have to pay back the margin borrowed.

Initial Margin Requirement

When a customer wishes to set up a margin account with his broker, he cannot simply request that the entire account be given as a loan. Instead, there is some specific portion of the account which he must contribute himself, and it is this equity which is the initial margin requirement. These requirements are not merely stipulated by brokerage firms, either, but are subject to government regulation. The initial margin requirement, as determined by Regulation T of the Financial Reserve Board is 50%. Different brokerage firms are free to establish their own initial margin requirement levels in excess of this percentage.

Margin Requirements for Short Sale Accounts

Since short sales involve the selling of stocks which an investor does not own (so that he can buy them back cheaper and return the stocks to their owner, pocketing the difference), there are stricter margin requirements. Whereas ordinary margin accounts have margin requirements of 50% (and long positions also have 50% requirements), short sale accounts, according to Regulation T requirements, have margin requirements of 150%. If an investor engages in a short sale for $5,000, then the margin requirement for his short sale account is $7,500.

Margin Accounts

Margin accounts are brokerage accounts in which the customer purchases securities using cash he borrowed from the broker.

- Since purchasing securities on credit is a riskier venture for the broker than a customer who purchases them with his own cash, it is necessary for the broker to approve any clients wishing to do so. Moreover, customers will generally be required to offer securities and cash as collateral. Brokerage firms will also have restrictions on what kind of accounts can be margin accounts, as well as what kind of securities can be purchased in margin accounts.

- Margin accounts require a certain portion of the account to be owned by the client, not the broker. If the value of certain stocks drops, then the client might be required to place more cash in the account or to sell off some of the securities. At one time, prior to the stock market crash of 1929, investors could buy stocks with only ten percent down. After the crash and after much blame for the crash was placed on speculators, the rule was changed in order to reduce the leverage and risk in margin trading. Currently, investors must put at least fifty percent of the stock price down in cash. To open an account, they must be approved based on their credit history. For their first purchase on margin, they must use at least $2,000.

Portfolio Margin Accounts and Day Trading Accounts

Portfolio margin accounts are a type of margin account where the initial margin requirement differs according to the particular risk of the portfolio. Whereas Regulation T requires all margin accounts to have an initial margin requirement of at least 50%, portfolio margin requirements can be much lower, perhaps between 15% and 20%. However, while the margin requirement is low, customers wishing to have a portfolio margin account must have a specific (and high) absolute amount of equity, usually $150,000. The portfolio margin is calculated according to the Options Clearing Corporation's (OCC's) Customer Portfolio Margin system.

Day trading accounts are especially risky margin accounts used to make a very high number of trades per day, making a profit or loss off of the small upticks and downticks in the daily price. Because of the extremely risky nature of day trading, the rules with respect to margin trading are a bit different when it comes to clients who wish to day trade. For one thing, day traders must always have at least $25,000 in equity in their account if they wish to day trade. If they don't meet this requirement, they are not allowed to day trade. And, unlike regular margin traders, their buying power isn't twice the SMA; instead, it is four times the equity in their account above the twenty-five percent maintenance minimum, which is called maintenance margin excess.

Hypothecation and Rehypothecation of Marginable Securities

Margin in an investment account is typically collateralized by the securities that are in the investment account. Hypothecation refers to the act of the client pledging marginable securities as collateral for margin given by the broker/dealer. In the event that the customer cannot repay the margin balance, their hypothecated securities may be taken as payment. Rehypothecation deals with the securities firm submitting hypothecated securities to a bank to collateralize a bank loan that will fund the margin account after the client has given the securities for collateral on their margin account. According to Regulation U, broker/dealers may pledge only up to 140% of their customer's securities as collateral for the margin loan.

Risk Disclosure That Must Be Given to Customers with Margin Accounts

Customers who wish to open margin accounts must receive the margin risk disclosure document prior to account opening. After the initial submission of the document to the customer, the document must be resubmitted to the client on an annual basis. Many of the risks associated with margin investing are contained within the document. Among those listed are the amplification of eventual losses by the client if the value of a security bought on margin decreases, the variability of the interest rate (tied to the broker call rate) on the margin account, the ability of the margin issuer to increase their margin requirements without notifying the customer prior to doing so, the inability of the client to choose the securities that may be sold if they cannot satisfy a maintenance call, the fact that extension of time for them to meet a maintenance call is at the discretion of the margin issuer, and that it is possible for the investor to lose more money than they deposited.

Marginable

The term *marginable* is defined as a security that may be pledged to collateralize the margin of a margin account. Not all securities are marginable or eligible to be purchased on margin. Regulation T governs which securities are marginable and which are not. Securities that are marginable and may be purchased on margin include warrants, exchange-traded stocks and bonds, stocks traded via the NASDAQ, and over-the-counter issues that have been approved by the Federal Reserve Board. Non-marginable securities that may not be purchased on margin include insurance contracts (life, annuities), options based on calls and puts, stock rights, and over-the-counter issues that have not been approved by the Federal Reserve board. Initial offerings and mutual funds are not eligible to be purchased on margin, but are considered marginable after they have been held for 30 days.

Differentiation of Treatment for Various Types of Securities and Accounts Regarding Margin

While some securities are specifically eligible and ineligible for margin use under Regulation T, some securities are exempt from Regulation T's government. For securities exempt from Regulation T's rules, the FINRA member firm sets their own rules regarding their treatment in a margin account. These guidelines must at least be in line with FINRA's minimum requirements, but many firms will often institute more stringent standards than FINRA requires to help guarantee compliance with policy. Securities to which Regulation T does not apply are bills, notes, and bonds issued by the United States government, debt issued by government agencies (FNMA, GNMA), and securities issued by United States municipalities.

Non-qualified investment accounts are typically the only type of investment account deemed suitable for margin. Qualified retirement accounts are usually off-limits for margin, since the risk associated with margin is high and the funds in the retirement account are critical to the customer's future security.

Securities Exchange Commission and Financial Industry Regulatory Authority Rules Regarding Margin Requirements and Calls

Regulation T was established by the Federal Reserve Board to help regulate the use of margin accounts. According to Regulation T, if an investor makes a purchase on margin, they must deposit at least 50% of the market value of the purchase within five business days of the purchase. If the customer so chooses, they may elect to deposit an amount larger than 50%, but it must be at least 50%. Additionally, the 50% must be at least $2,000. If the margin purchase is $3,000, the client must deposit at least $2,000 even though it is greater than 50%.

If a customer does not have a sufficient position in the account for 50% of the margin, the margin will be called. The customer must deposit the required amount within five days. This may be done with cash or by providing marginable securities that have at least twice the value of the called amount.

Short Sales

Short selling is the practice of an investor borrowing a security that they do not own and selling that security in hopes that the price of the security will decrease and they can buy it for less than they sold it, and return the security to the lender and keep the difference. Short sales are only allowed in margin accounts. Short selling is a valid investing strategy, but some unethical parties may also use it to manipulate the markets by selling large amounts of a stock short to create the illusion of a selloff and drive the price down. Market manipulation is illegal in any form, and subject to prosecution. When a short sale is made, the broker/dealer must first be sure that the security can be borrowed. This is referred to as locating a borrowable stock. After a stock is located, it can be borrowed from multiple sources such as lending firms and other customers' margin accounts.

Day Trading in Margin Accounts

An investor that buys and sells the same security on the same day to try to make a short-term gain is called a day trader. Even though gains may be small, a high volume of small gains may result in significant return. An investor who places more than three trades in five business days is called a pattern day trader. According to FINRA regulations, pattern day traders must keep at least $25,000 in equity in their margin accounts. They must also maintain a 25% minimum equity balance in their account. Pattern day traders may use 400% of the amount of equity in their account as buying power, but this equity must be that equity that exceeds the 25% rule. So a margin account with a $100,000 margin balance must have $25,000 in equity. If there is $26,000 in equity in the account, the trader has $4,000 in buying power (400% of $26,000–$25,000).

Basic Knowledge of Settlement

Elements of a Trade That Must Be Compared Between the Buyer and Seller in a Transaction Before the Trade Can Be Settled

Before a trade can be settled, the buyer of the security and the seller of the security must agree that the trade has been reported accurately. Both parties must agree by whom the trade will be reported (thus making it a buy or sell order), which security has been traded, the contra firm for the transaction, the number of securities being transacted, the price at which the order will be executed, and any accrued interest that might be necessary. Comparison of trades help both parties ensure that trade breaks do not occur. The parties may use the Automated Confirmation Transaction Service (ACT) to complete the comparison of trades electronically (usually the most efficient method), or they may do it via a clearing firms purchase sales department.

Regular Way Settlement

The majority of securities follow "regular way" rules for settlement. Regular way is most easily described by the faux formula T+1, where T stands for the trade date and 1 is the number of business days following the trade date. A trade placed on Monday would settle one day after the trade was placed, or Tuesday. (This used to be T+2 but was changed to T+1 effective May 28, 2024.) A trade placed on Monday would settle two days after the trade was placed, or Wednesday. There are a few securities, however, that do not settle in the regular way. Money market instruments settle the same day that they are transacted to ensure the liquidity for which they are used.

Settlement Service Providers

Due to the exclusive use of paper to clear, settle, and register securities, Wall Street firms became grossly inefficient, especially as the volume of trading expanded. To help the markets become more efficient, the Depository Trust & Clearing Corporation (DTCC) was established. The DTCC allowed for a standardized and automated process to be established to assist in clearing securities. The slow processes necessitated by the use of paper were no longer an obstacle.

The DTCC has ten subsidiaries. They are the National Securities Clearing Corporation, Fixed Income Clearing Corporation, the depository trust company, Avox Limited, EuroCCP Limited, The Warehouse Trust Company LLC, DTCC Deriv/SERV LLC, DTCC Derivatives Repository Limited, DTCC Solutions LLC, and DTCC Loan/SERV LLC. The services that DTCC offers through itself and these subsidiaries are Automated Customer Account Transfer Services (ACATS), trade comparison and reporting, Continuous Net Settlement, Stock Borrow Program, and settlement services.

Cash Settlement

Using cash settlement, which is also known as same day settlement, the seller must deliver the securities, and the buyer must pay for the securities, on the day the trade is executed. If the trade takes place before 2:00 p.m. ET, then settlement must take place by 2:30 p.m. If the trade takes place after 2:00 p.m., it must be settled within thirty minutes.

Repurchase Agreements

Repurchase agreements are used by firms as a means of raising liquidity without being required to permanently sell an asset. In a repurchase agreement, sometimes called a "repo agreement," a financial services firm enters into an agreement with another company that agrees to buy their securities and sell them back to them later at a higher price. While repo agreements have many characteristics in common with loans, the party receiving funding in a repo agreement actually sells the security instead of using it to collateralize a loan.

The two entities that are part of the repo agreements clear the agreement through the Fixed Income Clearing Corporation. The security underlying the repo agreement will be sent via FedWire (the Federal Reserve's electronic transfer service) to the purchasing company no later than 3:30 pm Eastern Time of the day that the repo transaction is executed.

Continuous Net Settlement

Continuous net settlement is an electronic accounting service provided by the Depository Trust and Clearing Company to provide clearing for multiple types of securities including stocks, bonds, unit investment trusts, and others. Trading between dealers results in large, usually complex orders. These trades are cleared through the National Securities Clearing Corporation (NSCC). The NSCC nets all of the trades between firms on a per security basis to facilitate delivery and settlement, thus participating in "continuous net settlement." Continuous net settlement streamlines the process of delivering and settling large trades, and avoids long delays associated with paper settlement that can be made even longer with such large orders.

"Don't Know" Trades and "Don't Know" Orders

A "don't know," or DK, status is appended to an interdealer trade in the event that either side of a trade that is submitted to the Automated Confirmation Transaction Service does not agree with one of the details of the transactions. For example, if a trade is placed and one of the parties does not agree with the reporting as to price, quantity, or some other aspect of the trade, that party will claim that it does not recognize the trade by marking it "don't know."

The "don't know" status may also be attached to a trade on the retail side of trading. DKs are usually attached to trades when there is a wrong or incomplete account number or other wrong information on a trade ticket.

Process by Which a FINRA Member May Buy in or Close out a Failed or Incomplete Trade

In the event of failure to delivery securities on a confirmed trade, the purchaser of the securities has several options to complete or close the order. If the purchaser in the transaction does not receive the transacted securities by the settlement date, they may close out the order on the third business day after the settlement date. The purchaser may then execute a "buy-in" and purchase the undelivered security from another source. The purchaser must give the seller a two-business-day notice before doing this. If a buy-in causes a loss to be incurred, the firm that failed to deliver on the original purchase must bear the loss.

Conversely, if the seller fails to pay for delivered securities (by regular settlement), the selling firm may sell the securities to another party. This is referred to as a "sellout." Again, if a loss is incurred because of failure to pay, the original buyer will be responsible for bearing the loss.

Status of a FINRA Member's Capital Assets When a Customer Fails to Deliver a Security and the Process of Aging a Failed Delivery

In the event that a customer fails to deliver sold securities by the settlement date, the FINRA member may place the market value of the undelivered securities on their books as a capital asset, but it must be marked as "failed to deliver." The failed delivery may remain on the books as an asset, but if it has not been received within five days of the original settlement date it will be considered an "aged security fail." Aged security fails may remain on the books, but no longer at the full value of the assets that should have been received. The value of aged securities fails is reduced by 15% for capital purposes, but the firm is still owed the full quantity of securities purchased.

Customer Account Statements

The Financial Industry Regulatory Authority (FINRA) obligates its members to send quarterly statements of account. Firms may choose to do so more frequently. If there is activity (transactions, interest received, dividends received, funds moving in and out of the account) in a given month that falls on a month other than the end of the quarter, a statement must be sent that month as well. The firm must also inform the client of free credit balances, or cash balances in their account that are not swept to money markets. Per regulation, the statement must recommend that the customer report any part of the statement with which they may have an issue to their broker/dealer as soon as possible. At the beginning of the year, the FINRA member must provide the customer with a statement detailing all of the account activity from the previous year. This statement, form 1099, will assist the clients with their tax preparation.

Confirmations

Customer Confirmations

Customer confirmations are notices of a customer's transaction(s) that must be delivered to the customer at or before the settlement date of the transaction. With the adoption of the T+1 settlement cycle for most securities, settlement is ordinarily one business day after the trade date.

Customer confirmations must include (1) the account number of the customer, (2) the ID number of the registered representative, (3) the trade date, (4) the type of transaction (bought or sold—BOT or SLD), (5) number of shares or the par value of bonds in the transaction, (6) the yield (if bonds are transacted), (7) the CUSIP ID number, (8) the dollar price of the security transacted, (9) the total amount of money paid or received, excluding commission, (10) the commission total, and (11) the net amount, that is, the amount the customer paid or received when the commission is taken into account, and when accrued interest is taken into account for bonds.

SEC and FINRA Rules Regarding Customer Confirmations

Confirmation of transactions (SEC Rule 10b-10) - broker/dealers must disclose certain information to the customer in writing at or before the completion of a transaction. This disclosure must contain specific information including the date and time of the transaction; the identity, price, and number of shares; agency disclosure of the broker/dealer; disclosure of any odd-lot differential fee paid for by the customer; and certain other disclosures for debt securities. There are some exceptions to the Rule such as certain transactions that are part of an investment company plan.

Customer confirmations (FINRA Rule 2232) - a member is to send to the customer a written notification at or before the completion of a transaction.

Trade Confirmations

Trade confirmations are summaries and confirmations of transactions for the customer's benefit. Trade confirmations must list the settlement date, the amount of the transaction, the date of the trade, the account number in which the trade was transacted, the identification number of the registered representative who facilitated the trade, whether it was a buy or sale, the security that was transacted along with its CUSIP (if applicable), any yield that the security may provide, the price per security, any commissions paid, and the total (or net) cost of the trade including all applicable expenses.

Confirmations must be sent at or prior to completion of the trade. The settlement date is considered the completion of the trade. If the customer provides consent, the broker/dealer may send confirmations electronically, but the customer must still have the option of requesting a paper confirmation.

Non-Trade Confirmations and Third-Party Activity Notices

Each time a transaction occurs within an account that is not related to trading activities, the customer must still be sent a confirmation. Non-trading activities that trigger confirmations include sending wires to and from foreign bank accounts, movement of stock within the account via physical stock certificates, and other similar activities. These activities warrant confirmations, but generate non-trade confirmations because no securities transaction was actually made.

Confirmations are also sent to customers in the event of third-party activity. Such activity may include payments to third parties or activity related to the management of the account by parties unaffiliated with the customer's broker/dealer.

Prospectus Delivery Requirements for Initial Public Offering

When a customer decides to buy a security or a registered representative sells a security to the customer that is relatively new to the market, the FINRA member sponsoring the sale must ensure that the customer receives the security's prospectus. For securities that have recently undergone initial public offering, or IPO, (in which all of the primary buyers received a prospectus), the prospectus must be delivered with the security for 25 days following the IPO if the security is

NASDAQ listed. If the security is to be traded via the pink sheets, the prospectus must be provided for 90 days following the IPO. In the event the issuer of an IPO makes an additional offering, NASDAQ listed stocks are only delivered with prospectus if they're purchased from the issuer. Pink sheet listed stocks must continue to provide the prospectus for an additional 40 days.

Tax Reporting

Relationship Between Cost Basis and Capital Gains

The cost basis of a security is the total cost of a security adjusted by outside influences that may have an impact on the final total cost paid. Commissions paid to a broker can serve to raise the cost basis of an investment. Other events, such as stock splits, may also affect the cost basis of an investment.

Capital gains or losses occur when an investor sells a capitalized asset, such as stocks and bonds. To determine the capital gain or loss, the investor need only subtract the cost basis from the sales price. A capital gain must be added to the investor's income for tax consideration, while capital losses may be written off their income, up to $3,000 per year for capital losses. Long-term and short-term capital gains are taxed differently; long-term gains receive favorable tax treatment. Any investment sold after it is held more than one year is considered long-term.

Special Tax Withholding Rules Regarding TEFRA, Mutual Funds, and Employer-Sponsored Qualified Retirement Plans

TEFRA, an acronym for the Tax Equity and Fiscal Responsibility Act, established mandatory withholding of 10% from dividend gains received from securities that are held in accounts that do not have a tax identification number (TIN) on file. Similarly, a customer that does not have a Social Security number (SSN) or TIN on file and invests in mutual will be subject to a mandatory withholding of 31% of any distributions.

Employer-sponsored retirement plans are subject to 20% mandatory withholding on any distribution. Distributions to roll the plan over to a new plan or a direct transfer to another IRA plan are exempt from this withholding rule, since the funds are not actually being withdrawn.

Taxation for Dividends

When dividends are distributed as cash, they are subject to taxation as well. And just as capital gains can be taxed less if they are classified as long-term, so also dividends can be taxed differently, depending on whether they are qualified or non-qualified.

Qualified dividends are dividends which can be taxed at the (lower) long-term capital gains rate. To count as qualified dividends, they must be disbursed by a US corporation or a qualifying foreign corporation, and they must be held by the investor for at least 60 days within the 121-day period that begins 60 days prior to the ex-dividend date.

Non-qualified dividends are taxed at the investor's ordinary income rate.

Tax Implications for Stocks Acquired Through Conversion

If stock is acquired through conversion, such as by exercising the conversion feature on convertible bonds, then any gain or loss acquired through the conversion is *not immediately relevant* to capital gains or losses. Instead, the basis of the stocks is equal to the value of the debt at the point of conversion. This basis is then the reference point for determining future capital gains or losses on that stock.

For example, if a convertible bond with a basis of $1,000 is converted into 20 shares of stock selling at that date for $55 apiece, then the basis of the stock investment will still be $1,000 (effectively $50 per share), and the investor will recognize no capital gain or loss at that point. (That is, he will *not* recognize a gain of $100 at the date of conversion, even though the stock is valued at $1,100 and the bond at $1,000.) However, if the investor were to then sell the stocks at $60 per share one year later, then that would be taxable event upon his capital gain of $10 per share sold.

The *holding period* for the stock begins at the date of the debt issuance, not at the date of conversion.

Average Basis Method for Mutual Funds

Mutual funds make the calculation of capital gains and losses to be much trickier, since the customer is often unaware of all the securities transactions executed by the fund manager. One common method is the average basis method.

According to this method, the total money paid for shares is divided by the total number of shares to give the investor an average basis per share. Then, whenever he sells any shares, the basis is lowered accordingly: the quantity of shares decreases, but the basis per share remains the same.

If an investor purchased 100 shares for $15/share two years and 100 shares for $20/share last year, then if he sold 150 shares today, the cost basis to which he would compare the selling price would be $2,625 (150 shares x $17.50/share). The remaining cost basis on his other 50 shares would be $875 (50 shares x $17.50/share).

It can be difficult to determine whether capital gains are short- or long-term with average basis methods. To solve this, there used to be *average cost single category* (ACSC) and *average cost double category* methods (ACDC), but ACDC has been discontinued by the IRS since April 2011.

FIFO, LIFO, and Specific Share Identification

With the first in, first out (FIFO) method for valuing one's stocks, given a list of how many shares were bought or sold on which day (and at what price), the investor assumes for simplicity's sake that any shares sold are the oldest ones he possesses. If he bought 100 shares at $15 per share two years ago and 100 shares at $20 per share last year, then if he sells 150 shares today, it will be as if he sold $2,500 worth of shares: (100 shares x $15/share) + (50 shares x $20/share). $2,500 would be the basis against which he compares the selling price to determine capital gains or losses.

Under the last in, first out (LIFO) method, the newest stocks are assumed to be the ones sold. In the above example, the cost basis of the sold shares would be $2,750: (100 shares x $20/share) + (50 shares x $15/share).

Specific share identification involves the most work, since the investor (or mutual fund manager) must keep track of the buying and selling prices for every transaction of stock at the time it was transacted. The benefit of this is that it tends to reduce one's taxes.

Other methods are *high cost, first out* (HCFO) and *low cost, first out* (LCFO), where the basis is determined by the relative prices of the acquired shares, not the time at which they were purchased.

Wash Sales

The IRS generally permits investors to offset investment gains with capital losses up to $3,000 a year. However, a capital loss may not be used to offset gains if the investor, within thirty days after taking the loss, then buys the same security, or one that is "substantially identical," which would include warrants, rights, options, and convertible bonds in the same stock. If the investor purchases the same security or a substantially identical one within thirty days of the loss, it is considered a wash sale, and cannot be factored in with net capital losses to offset gains or income.

Taxation of a Mutual Fund's Investor's Profits

The tax rate that a mutual fund investor pays depends on several different factors, and tax rates can be quite different, depending on how the profit being taxed was derived. Income from dividends is simply taxed at the 15 percent rate. But realized capital gains are divided into two categories, short-term and long-term. Long-term capital gains are capital gains realized from the sale of securities held for longer than a year, and they're taxed at the capital gains rate of 15 percent. Capital gains realized from the sale of securities held for less than a year are taxed at regular income tax rates.

Taxation of Bonds

Bondholders' income normally comes from the periodic interest payments of the bond. However, discounts and premiums make things slightly more complicated. For tax purposes, any discount on a bond has to be *accreted* (increased) on a straight-line basis over the bond's term; the annual accretion amount is then added to the investor's reported income on the bond. The opposite occurs for bonds purchased at a premium. Premiums are *amortized* (decreased), with the annual amortization amount being subtracted from the investor's reported income.

For example, suppose an investor purchased at 95 a 10-year bond with a face value of $1,000 and stated rate of 6%. The discount of $50 would be accreted at a rate of

$5 per year, and so the bondholder's reported income for each year would be $65 ($60 interest + $5 accretion).

Bonds that are originally issued at a discount are unsurprisingly called *original issue discounts* (OIDs).

Taxation of Municipal Bonds

Gains from investments on municipal bonds are ordinarily not taxed. Taxable municipal bonds can be issued if the purpose of the bond revenue has no clear public benefit, but most municipal bonds are tax-exempt.

This means not only that coupon payments are not taxed, but also that gains from original issue discount (OID) bonds are tax-exempt as well. Accretion on the discount of municipal OID bonds is treated as tax-exempt interest income.

Discounts on municipal bonds purchased in the secondary market are not even accreted. These are the only bonds whose discounts are not accreted.

Capital Gains and Losses on Bonds

Accretion of bond discounts and amortization of bond premiums affect not only reported income but also capital gains and losses on bonds.

For example, suppose a bondholder purchased at 95 a 10-year bond with a face value of $1,000 and stated rate of 6%. Suppose this bondholder sold the bond to another investor for 105, 5 years after the bond's issuance. If so, the capital gain on the sale would be $75—the difference between $1,050 (the selling price) and $975 (the $950 buying price plus $25 accretion over five years).

Tax-Equivalent Yield

The tax-equivalent yield is the yield that a taxable bond needs to have before taxes in order to achieve the same return as a nontaxable bond.

Tax-equivalent yield = (desired yield) / (1 – tax rate)

For example, if a nontaxable bond had a yield of 18% and the tax rate were 12%, then any taxable bonds, to be more valuable to the investor, would need to have a yield of 20.45% (18% / 88%).

Federal, State, and Local Taxation for Municipal Bonds

Investors need not pay any taxes on interest income from municipal bonds, although they may have to pay state or local taxes, depending on their laws.

US territories (including American Samoa, Guam, Puerto Rico, and the Virgin Islands) and federal districts (Washington, D.C.) are *triple tax-free* regarding municipal bonds. Bondholders don't have any federal, state, or local taxes to pay on interest.

Most states, but not all, are triple tax-free regarding municipal bonds for investors purchasing bonds issued within their own state.

Despite all these tax exemptions for interest income, capital gains from the sales of bonds is still taxable.

Prohibited Activities for Customer Accounts and Confirmations

Falsification and Withholding of Customer Documents

The Financial Industry Regulatory Authority (FINRA) expressly forbids the falsification of client documents such as statements and confirmations. Statements are particularly easy to falsify, since there is not an industry standard and each FINRA member creates their own. Members may attempt to allay customers' fears and keep their business by inflating their securities prices on the statement or on confirmations sent to the customer. This is in no case legal or ethical. Neither is it legal or ethical to withhold the statements or confirmation beyond the accepted time periods, such as trade settlement dates for confirmations. The only case in which holding documents is acceptable is in the event the customer supplies a written request to withhold these documents for up to two months if they're traveling within the United States or three months if traveling outside the United States.

Basic Knowledge of Books and Records

Retaining Books and Records for Customers and Firms

One of the duties of a broker for his customers is to retain various books and records. According to MSRB Rule G-8, these include records of original entry, account records, securities records, and subsidiary records, such as records for municipal securities in transfer, municipal securities to be validated, municipal securities borrowed or loaned, and municipal securities transactions not completed on the settlement date. The broker should also maintain records for put options and repurchase agreements, records for agency transactions, records for transactions as principal, records concerning primary offerings, and other records. Essentially, the broker should maintain a paper trail for all of his customer's substantial activity.

Reconciliation of a Firm's Accounting Records

When companies receive their bank statements, it is beneficial for them to check the statement against their own general ledger to ensure that the bank is posting payments and deposits in accordance with their records. This is known as a bank reconciliation. Per the Securities Exchange Commission (SEC), firms must post to their general ledger (GL) at least monthly and not more than ten business days after the month's end. Other SEC posting requirements include stock records (posted by the next business day), blotters (posted by the next business day), posting to the customer's ledger by the settlement date, the posting of transfer records within two business days after the transfer has been given to the agent, posting borrowed or loaned stock within two business days, posting discovered securities discrepancies within seven business days, posting loaned or borrowed cash within two business days, and posting delivery or receipt failures within two business days of settlement.

Records That Must Be Held

The Securities Exchange Commission regulates the records that must be established and maintained by FINRA members. Articles of partnership or incorporation, minutes from meetings of the major parties responsible for the business, books containing information of stock certificate transactions, and documents that establish the organization must be held for the life of the firm. Blotters, general ledgers, customer ledgers, stock records, and records of customers' accounts must be retained for six years. All other records that a FINRA member firm keeps must be retained for a minimum of three years. Exceptions to this rule are Suspicious Activity Reports, Form 104, and customer identity documentation; these must be retained for five years. Regardless of the time that the records are required to be held, the past two years must be kept on hand for easy access. Electronic storage is permissible so long as the storage method is not erasable.

Books and/or Records That Brokers and Dealers Are Required to Maintain

Blotters or other records of original entry - are to contain an itemized daily record of all purchases and sales of securities, all receipts and deliveries of securities, all receipts and disbursements of cash, as well as all other debits and credits.

Copies of customer confirmations - and copies of notices of all other debits and credits for accounts of customers.

Identification data on beneficial owners of all accounts - all cash and margin accounts are to have identification data including the name and address of the beneficial owner of the account.

Ledgers or other records reflecting all assets and liabilities - including income and expense and capital accounts.

Memorandum of each brokerage order given or received for the purchase or sale of securities (for customer and firm accounts) - whether executed or unexecuted. The memorandum is to show the terms and conditions; the account for which entered; the time the order was received; the time of entry; the price it was executed; the identity of any associated persons responsible for the account; the identity of the person who entered or accepted the order; and the time of execution or cancellation.

Memorandum of each purchase and sale for the account of the firm - including the price, the time of execution, and if the transaction was with a customer other than a broker or dealer, a memorandum of each order received showing the time of receipt, the terms and conditions; the identity of each associated person responsible for the account; and the identity of the person who entered or accepted the order.

Professional Conduct and Ethical Considerations

Employee Conduct

Process of Completing Registration with FINRA

To complete securities registration, the representative must first be sponsored by a firm that is a member of FINRA. After the person has obtained sponsorship, they must file Form U-4 and pass the exams ("Series" exams) that are applicable to their role at the firm. Form U-4 must be completed with the representative's name and address, residency history for the previous five years, ten years of employment history, and any accusations of criminal activity pertaining to the securities industry.

After registering with FINRA, the representative must register with other SROs with whom they intend to do business and with the states in which they intend to transact. An additional exam must be passed (Series 63 or 66) to transact business in a state. Registration with other SROs usually only involves paying the registration fee, since most SROs accept the FINRA exams.

Forms U-4 and U-5

While Form U-4 acts as the registration form for representatives applying to FINRA, there are also certain events that representatives are required to disclose on U-4. If the representative has been charged with, arrested for, and/or convicted of securities related fraud and crime, they must disclose it on the Disclosure Reporting Page of Form U-4. Form U-5 is used as the reporting vehicle when a representative will no longer be involved in the securities industry. In the event that the representative was terminated, the FINRA member must provide a copy of Form U-5 to the terminated employee and describe on U-5 why the employee was either terminated or allowed to resign. If the firm becomes cognizant of information that would change the U-5, they must file an amendment within 30 days and provide an amended copy to the terminated party.

In the event that a person files misleading or false information, or omits information of substance, their registration will be immediately invalidated regardless of their pass/fail status of their required exam. There may be other steps taken by the Financial Industry Regulator Authority (FINRA) and/or the Securities Exchange Commission (SEC), such as civil charges and fines.

FINRA, in order to help protect consumers from unscrupulous investment professionals, requires that individuals that are substantially involved in the administration of the securities industry be registered. Their registration implies an educational process that imparts the importance of following FINRA regulations. If an individual practices without registration, they (and any associated FINRA member) are liable to be subject to civil charges and fines, and to make restitution to customers for whom they transacted.

Continuing Education Requirements for Registered Persons

To ensure that registered persons stay abreast of matters of importance, and not simply study to pass the requisite exam, FINRA requires that all registered persons complete a certain amount of continuing education requirements to maintain their registration. FINRA continuing education consists of two portions. The regulatory element is created by FINRA and must be completed (via computerized training) within four months after their initial registration and every three years afterward. The firm element is created by the FINRA member. It must be completed annually by all registered employees of the firm. The firm element typically addresses recent relevant topics such as changes in laws, tax policies, and new dangers to customers such as scams and elder abuse.

Outside Business Activities and Outside Securities Accounts of Registered Individuals

The Financial Industry Regulatory Authority (FINRA) requires that registered persons notify their employing FINRA member if they are compensated in any form by another party for any activities performed other than investment-related activities. The employing FINRA member must then approve or disapprove the activity. If the activity would create a conflict of interest with the firm's customers or be potentially illegal or hazardous to the FINRA member's well-being, they will disallow the activity. Passive investment activities on the part of registered individuals do not require disclosure, although investment accounts held with another FINRA member must be disclosed to their employing FINRA firm.

Legality and Consequences of Trading Securities on Inside Information

Trading on non-public information, also called insider training, describes the act of an individual with inside information about a publicly traded company acting on that information. Once the information is made public, the insider may legally trade based on the information. Persons with inside information can vary widely. While it is most common for directors and officers of the company to have substantial non-public information, lower level employees may be privy to it, spouses of employees may also be aware, or even someone unconnected to the publicly traded company that obtains the information. None of the persons described above may trade on the information until it becomes public.

In no circumstances is trading on inside information legal or ethical. The Securities Exchange Commission (SEC) may penalize a party convicted of insider trading larger than three times the amount of profit that they made or lost due to their insider trading, or $1,000,000. If the SEC determines criminal intent in the insider trading, they may impose up to a $5,000,000 fine and twenty years in prison.

Code of Conduct a Registered Person Should Follow Regarding Selling Away

In the event that a registered person wishes to participate in a securities transaction not affiliated with his or her firm, known as selling away, the person is permitted to do so as long as he or she provides proper written notice to their employing firm. Proper notice includes a detailed description of the transaction, whether the representative will be compensated in any manner for participating in the transaction, and the representative's part in the transaction.

As with outside activities, if the representative is to be compensated in the transaction, their employee FINRA member must approve the activity and enter the transaction on their books. Also, similarly to outside business activities, if the employer disallows the transaction, the representative may not participate therein.

Restrictions on the Purchasing of Initial Public Offerings

The Financial Industry Regulatory Authority (FINRA) expressly forbids broker/dealers registered with FINRA from selling shares of initial public offerings (IPOs) to restricted persons, or to accounts in which restricted persons have a significant interest. This rule is in place to protect customers that may wish to participate in the IPO, but are unable to because the restricted persons have had unfair access to the IPO shares. Persons considered restricted for this purpose are FINRA member firms, a party owning more than 9% of a FINRA member firm, financial consultant and/or accountants, employees of FINRA member firms, representatives of the firm that is underwriting the issue, and portfolio managers. Also included in the definition of restricted person is any immediate family member of any of the above-mentioned parties. Extended family members that reside with restricted persons are also considered restricted.

Deception in the Sale of Securities and Improper Use and Guarantees of Customers' Accounts

The use of deceptive practices on the part of the registered person is a direct violation of this duty. Unethical representatives may manipulate or coerce customers into buying unsuitable securities out of a desire for the highest payout per dollar. This is a double violation of the representative's duty and leaves the person liable to lawsuits that do not have a maximum limit. A further violation of a representative's duty may occur when the person misuses the customers' funds to which they have been entrusted. This often takes the form of the advisor using the customers' funds for personal uses and not returning it.

Registered persons may not share in accounts with customers unless prior approval by the employing firm is given. The sharing in the account must be proportionate. If the representative takes a disproportionate share of loss in the account, this could be viewed as guaranteeing against loss, which is expressly prohibited.

Prohibition Against Paying Commissions to Unregistered Persons

Only persons registered with FINRA may accept payment and commissions for sales of securities executed (excluding trading exempt securities). There are instances in which persons may wish to pay commissions to an unregistered person; this should be avoided at all times. Such situations may include a bank teller sending a high net-worth individual to a registered person, and the representative giving the teller money as an incentive and a thank-you. As innocuous as a situation like this may seem, it is not allowed under FINRA regulations.

Providing a non-FINRA member with a member discount may also be construed as a commission. This is only allowable if the person discounted is associated with a FINRA member. For these purposes, members of FINRA that have been suspended or barred are not considered members.

Relationships

Acceptable Methods of Communicating with Customers and the General Public

When employees of FINRA member firms communicate with their customers, FINRA requires that records of the communication be retained. This includes incoming and outgoing mail. If the correspondence is a form letter going to multiple parties, it is considered group correspondence and may be subject to review by a registered principal (RP). Firms that do not require review by RPs must train their representatives regarding FINRA compliance of group correspondence and note the training in writing.

Advertisements and sales literature must be approved by an RP and filed with FINRA within 10 days of use. Regardless of the form the communication takes, whether electronic or physical, it must be retained for potential review by FINRA.

FINRA members must take great care to protect the customer's personal information, especially during correspondence. When personal information is involved, privacy envelopes should be used in physical communication, and electronic communication should be over secure or encrypted lines.

Gifting

The gifting of a very expensive item to a customer of a firm can be viewed as guaranteeing against loss or reimbursing losses. Both of these instances are illegal and unethical. Additionally, using expensive gifts as an inducement to buy securities is unethical and illegal. FINRA has explicit rules regarding gifting stated in FINRA Rule 3220. Associates may give up to $100 in value to each customer in a calendar year. Similarly, they may give or receive only $100 in value to other associates of other member firms. This is to prevent funneling business to other firms, which may not be in the customer's best interest. Exceptions to Rule 3220 include personal gifts, promotional items (i.e., pens, inexpensive desk decorations), and items that honor business deals (i.e., plaques) even if these articles surpass $100 in value.

Non-Cash Compensation in the Form of Business Entertainment

Some FINRA members firms, such as open-end mutual funds companies, provide meals, tickets to entertainment venues, or reimbursement for travel and other expenses associate with attended conferences and seminars as inducement to sell their product. For the investment companies to provide these incentives, the representative that accepts the compensation must have their firm's permission to attend the meeting, the firm must keep a record of any non-cash compensation that the representative receives, they do not receive reimbursement for recreational activities while at the meeting, the location of the meeting is in line with the purpose of the meeting, reimbursement is not dependent upon a sales goal being reached, and there is no reimbursement for the representative's spouse to attend.

Reporting Political Contributions

Registered persons of FINRA member firms are limited as to how much they may contribute to a political candidate per election. The Municipal Securities Rulemaking Board (MSRB) is the self-regulatory organization (SRO) that established Rule G-37 that governs certain political contributions made by registered persons. FINRA applies this rule to its members. Each registered person may contribute up to $250 per election.

All contributions that are covered by Rule G-37 are reported on Form G-37. The information on Form G-37 part I includes detailed information about the individual recipient and detailed information regarding the contribution to the recipient. Form G-37-part II lists information about contributions made to political parties, and detailed information regarding the contributions. The contributions are listed by the state in which the contributions were made. Form G-37 is filed quarterly.

Customer Privacy

Confidentiality of the Customer's Records and Non-Public Personal Information

The Gramm-Leach-Bliley Act established Regulation SP that governs the way in which customers' private records and information must be protected. Regulation SP requires that firms establish a policy for all employees to follow that will protect their customers' non-public personal information. This policy must cover all aspects of record retention including relatively recent technological advances (such as wi-fi) that may present new ways for criminals to attempt to steal information. The privacy policy must be given to each new customer when they open an account. Firms may share non-public personal information to other legitimate third parties with interest unless the customer requests that they do not do it. Information may be shared between departments of the firm without special disclosure, since the departments are part of the FINRA firm that services the customer.

Objecting Beneficial Owner and Nonobjecting Beneficial Owner

Beneficial ownership describes a situation in which the owner of a security elects for their security to be registered in street name (the name of their broker) for convenience sake, while remaining the actual owner or "beneficial owner." A non-objecting beneficial owner, sometimes referred to as a NOBO, does not object to the broker sharing personal information with the issue of the security that they purchased in street name. The issuer typically uses this information to send the beneficial owner documents related to their securities such as proxy votes and annual reports. An objecting beneficial owner (OBO) is one that elects for their broker not to send personal information to the issuer of the security that they bought in street name. In this case, to obtain documents and information from the issue, the OBO must rely on their broker who is the registered owner.

Red Flags

A red flag is activity in a customer's account that may indicate misuse of the owner's money. This misuse may be on the part of the customer, such as money laundering, or on the part of the broker/dealer, like improper treatment of the customer's money by their registered representative.

FINRA requires that its members review accounts to monitor for red flags. This is most easily done with the use of exception reports. Exception reports compile lists of accounts that have recently experienced suspicious activity and make the information available to the FINRA member in one report so that they may focus on those accounts to determine if the red flags are an indication of actual misuse of customer funds.

Privacy Regulations

A number of privacy regulations govern broker-dealers. Financial institutions are prohibited from disclosing nonpublic personal information about any customers to third parties not affiliated with the customer (except in certain circumstances where the institution informs the customer and he does not opt out), and they are required to provide customers with a notice of the institution's privacy policies and practices. Institutions must also develop processes and standards for the protection of their customers' information. The bulk of these regulations are contained in Regulation S-P, issued by the SEC to protect customers from the risk of identity theft or fraud and from unauthorized access to their private information.

Importance of Escalating Complaints and/or Potential Red Flags

Recognizing a Red Flag or Complaint

Complaints are easily recognized. Complaints occur when customers inform the firm in writing if they take issue directly or tangentially with a securities transaction. Resolutions of complaints are obtained when the customer and FINRA firm agree on the resolution. In this case, the firm need only keep a record of the complaint, and no further escalation is required. If the firm and the customer cannot come to an agreement, the case will be escalated to FINRA for arbitration.

Red flags are usually identified via an exceptions report. It is vital that each red flag is investigated immediately to prevent fraud in a customer's account. The escalation process involves contacting the proper personnel until the issue is resolved. Such persons may include the account representative and/or registered principal among others.

Handling Customer Complaints Properly with FINRA

Complaints, to be official, must be in writing. FINRA has different proceedings for handling customer complaints: formal and informal. The customer making the complaint decides whether to pursue formal or informal proceedings.

If the customer decides to pursue formal proceedings to resolve his complaint, then the complaint must be resolved according to FINRA's code of procedure. According to this, the District Business Conduct Committee (DBCC) maintains first jurisdiction over complaints, and if the customer is dissatisfied with the DBCC's handling of the issue, he can appeal the outcome to the FINRA Board of Governors and even up to the Supreme Court.

If the customer decides to pursue informal proceedings, then the complaint can be resolved according to FINRA's code of arbitration. According to this, at least two arbiters will participate in an informal hearing, and their decision will be binding and not open to appeal. Arbitration can be pursued not only by customers, but by any members of FINRA, including complaints that RRs might have with broker-dealers.

Mediation is also available for complaints, where an independent third party provides a nonbinding resolution to the matter.

Broker/Dealer Supervision and Control

Need for Segregation of Functions and Supervision Among Departments

Although departments within FINRA member firms work closely to achieve the same goal, methods and needs can vary greatly between departments. Because the departments require varying areas of expertise, and cross-supervision can result in conflicts of interest, segregating duties and supervision is required to maintain an ethical and efficient firm. Conflicts of interest may arise when an employee in a department provides a negative review of another department. That employee may refrain from honesty if they fear retribution from the supervisor of the other department. Information barriers help prevent conflicts of interest by restricting the flow of information between departments. Information shared between departments may provide employees in each group with opportunities to take advantage of inside information.

Control of Access to Information, Buildings and Offices, and Computer Files and Systems

To ensure that customers' information is secure, FINRA member firms should implement privacy policies to aid in restricting access to information by unauthorized parties. This can partially be accomplished by restricting access to the firm's offices by unauthorized people. Since some people have access to the facilities that are not employees of the FINRA member firm, such as cleaning crews, further measures other than restricting building access must be taken to prevent access. Such steps include (but are not limited to) securing files in locked cabinets and locking desks that contain sensitive information. Further, if the firm retains sensitive information on computers and networks, access to the network and computer should be restricted with an entitlement policy, a unique username and password log-in. Entitlement policies also refer to keys to the facility and unique codes that may activate/deactivate alarms and unlock doors.

Compliance with FINRA Regulations Regarding Written Supervisory Procedures (WSP)

As required by regulation, FINRA member firms should develop, in writing, supervisory procedures that govern the behavior of the firm's employees in such a way that their behavior is in compliance with their Self-Regulatory Organization (SRO) and the Securities Exchange Commission (SEC). The member firm is required to keep a physical copy of their WSP in their offices along with a copy of the FINRA manual and make them available to customers at their request. A senior ranking officer of the firm must attest to FINRA annually by April 1 that they have developed a WSP. Updating occurs as frequently as necessary, but the WSP should be updated at least annually. Almost without exception, WSPs are updated more frequently than annually.

Business Continuity Plans

Business continuity plans (BCP) are contingency plans upon which businesses rely in the event of a major event that may substantially interrupt business operations. FINRA requires that each of their member firms have a BCP in place. BCPs should provide for the recovery of data, substitute forms of communications between the FINRA member and its employees and customers, a method by which the firm's customers may access their assets in the event of business closure, methods by which the firm may remain in contact with regulators, and a secondary facility for employees. A written BCP must be provided to the firm's customers when the customer opens an account and at any time the customer requests it. The BCP should also be posted on the firm's website for customer viewing.

Series 99 Practice Test

Want to take this practice test in an online interactive format?
Check out the online resources page, which includes interactive practice questions and much more:
mometrix.com/resources719/series99

1. An investor owns 75 shares of 7 percent preferred stock in company TRJ. What would be the annual income on this investor's investment?

a. $7
b. $5,250
c. $525
d. $52,500

2. Which of the following is NOT true of a stock dividend?

a. stock price of an individual share will increase in order to reflect the increase in the number of outstanding shares
b. utilized by a company that wants to provide a reward to its shareholders without consuming cash
c. investors will receive a number of additional shares based on the number currently owned prior to the dividend
d. overall market value is unchanged after distribution of it

3. Which of the following describes a situation that would motivate a corporation to repurchase its own shares?

a. it would like to fund an acquisition with the shares
b. it is seeking to retain control over the company
c. it is making an effort to cause an increase in the company's earnings per share
d. all of the above

4. Corporation MDS provides its shareholders with a quarterly dividend of $1.50. Given a current market price of $32.50, what would the current yield of this stock be?

a. 18.5 percent
b. 4.6 percent
c. 21.7 percent
d. 5.4 percent

5. An investor owns DSY 5 percent convertible preferred stock and would like to convert it into DSY common stock at a conversion price of $5 per share. How many shares of DSY common stock will this investor receive once converted?

a. 100
b. 1
c. 20
d. none of the above

6. Which of the following is NOT true of the book value of a corporation?

a. dividing a company's book value amount by the number of its outstanding common shares will result in a per-share book value
b. calculated by adding a company's assets and its liabilities together
c. defined as a company's liquidation value
d. all of the above are true

7. Which of the following is NOT true regarding the rights of stockholders?

a. afforded the right to the company's residual assets post-bankruptcy, in an amount that's proportional to their investment in the company
b. afforded the right of inspection of the books and records of the company for which they own shares
c. afforded the right to be provided with a complete list of the company's shareholders
d. afforded the right to have access to portions of the company's confidential financial information

8. An investor owns 1,500 shares of HPE. The company will be paying a 3 percent stock dividend to all of its shareholders. How many more shares of HPE will this investor own as a result?

a. 5
b. 450
c. 45
d. unknown, need more information to determine

9. Preferred stock:

I. has no maturity date
II. is always nonvoting
III. provides for a priority claim over common stockholders for dividend distribution
IV. is interest rate sensitive

a. I. and III.
b. I., III., and IV.
c. I., II., III., and IV.
d. I., II., and III.

10. Which of the following are TRUE of equity?

I. at the point of maturity, the investor will receive its investment amount back
II. represents ownership in the company that issues it
III. creates a creditor relationship between the investor and the issuing corporation
IV. provides a means for a corporation to raise capital

a. II. only
b. III. and IV.
c. II. and IV.
d. II., III., and IV.

11. Which of the following is NOT true of callable preferred stock?

a. shares may be called during a rate decline in order to then sell new preferred shares with a lower fixed dividend rate
b. most often the shares are called at a premium to par
c. call protection provides for some delay past issuance in which the shares cannot be called by the company
d. the call feature is designed to benefit primarily the investor, not the company

12. An investor owns 250 shares of LYT at an original purchase price of $55.50 per share. Exactly one year later, he decides to sell all 250 shares at a current market price of $74.50. What would be the total profit that this investor would realize on this transaction?

a. $19.00
b. $4,750
c. $5,000
d. $18.50

13. All of the following are true of preferred stock EXCEPT:

a. provides for payment of semiannual dividends
b. represents ownership in the company
c. dividend is set at a fixed rate
d. company is not obligated to pay dividends to preferred stockholders

14. Stock that has been sold to investors and then purchased back by the issuing corporation is:

a. treasury stock
b. outstanding stock
c. authorized stock
d. issued stock

15. Which of the following is/are TRUE of a shareholder's preemptive right in relation to a rights offering?

I. rights may be sold to another investor interested in buying newly offered shares
II. the shareholder possesses the right to purchase newly offered shares at a discount
III. subscription price remains fixed for 35 days
IV. rights to purchase may be exercised by submitting payment and rights for shares

a. I., II., III., and IV.
b. I. and III.
c. I., II., and IV.
d. II. and IV.

16. Which of the following is NOT considered a type of security?

a. bond
b. fixed annuity
c. mutual fund
d. variable annuity

17. An investor owns 100 shares of 6 percent cumulative preferred stock in company RTS. The company has not paid dividends this year and for the past two years. How much is this investor owed in accumulated unpaid dividends?

a. $1,200
b. $6,000
c. $1,800
d. $180

18. An investor owns 650 shares of corporation PPG. There is an upcoming election in which this investor will be casting his vote. The election is for two of the corporation's board members and there are five candidates running. Under the statutory method of voting, what will be this investor's distribution of votes?

a. candidate #1: 650 votes, candidate #3: 650 votes
b. candidate #4: 650 shares
c. candidate #5: 1,300 shares
d. candidate #2: 325 votes, candidate #4: 325 votes

19. Which of the following are TRUE of an option seller?

I. income comes from the premium paid by the buyer of the option
II. enters into the option contract with the goal of having it exercised by the buyer
III. obligated to perform based on the terms of the option contract
IV. loses money upon expiration of the contract

a. II. and IV.
b. I., II., and III.
c. IV. only
d. I. and III.

20. Which of the following types of dispute resolution does NOT always end in a final binding decision regarding the issue being disputed?

a. simplified arbitration
b. minor rule violation (MRV) procedure
c. mediation
d. arbitration

21. Which of the following are TRUE of the Securities Investor Protection Corporation (SIPC)?

I. it will require a firm to conduct limited and very specific business upon having a trustee appointed for the purpose of liquidation
II. it is a private corporation
III. it will petition for the appointment of a trustee to liquidate the firm, should it fail to meet its minimum capital requirement
IV. broker-dealer membership is required if registered with the SEC

a. III. and IV.
b. I. and II.
c. II., III., and IV.
d. IV. only

22. A municipal finance professional (MFP) provides a donation of $350 to a candidate's election in which she is not eligible to vote. Which of the following is NOT a possible outcome to this situation?

a. the donation of $350 results in a violation of MSRB Rule G-38
b. the MFP's firm will not be able to participate in the business of municipal securities for that issuer for one year
c. the MFP's firm will not be able to participate in the business of municipal securities for that issuer for two years
d. the donation to a candidate for an election in which she is ineligible to vote results in a violation of MSRB Rule G-38

23. Of the following statements regarding institutional accounts and communications, which is NOT true?

a. institutional accounts have no minimum size requirements
b. due to most being larger in size, more laws are in place for the protection of these investors
c. member firms must maintain these communications for three years
d. government agencies are considered to be institutional investors

24. Regulation T regulates which of the following groups in their extension of credit for the purchase of securities?

a. financial institutions outside of banks and broker-dealers
b. banks
c. broker-dealers
d. all of the above

25. Which of the following is an example of a possible penalty to be handed down as a result of a finding of violation in a minor rule violation "formal" hearing?

a. suspension for up to six months
b. expulsion for up to five years
c. $2,500 fine
d. fine of whatever amount is deemed appropriate

26. All of the following are true of the definition of retail communications EXCEPT:

a. accessible to 25 retail investors or more over a 60-day period
b. includes sales literature
c. maintained by the member firm for three years
d. distributed electronically OR by hard copy

27. Which of the following is the debt issuer with the least amount of default or credit risk?

a. US government agencies
b. US government
c. municipal bonds
d. corporate bonds

28. Which of the following customer accounts will be fully covered by SIPC in the event of a broker-dealer failure that results in losses to the account?

a. securities: $310,000, cash: $200,000
b. securities: $275,000, cash: $275,000
c. securities: $145,000, cash: $350,000
d. securities: $325,000, cash: $165,000

29. An investor is seeking to be exempt from the penny stock cold call rule as an "established customer" with a certain firm. Which of the following is a requirement for qualifying her for that exemption?

a. three separate transactions, executed over three different days, involving three different penny stocks
b. three separate penny stock transactions, executed over three different days
c. three separate transactions, involving three different penny stocks, executed sometime over the previous 12 months
d. none of the above

30. Which of the following are TRUE of option contracts?

I. buyer is obligated to fulfill the contract
II. buyer under contract is provided the right to buy or sell a security
III. buyer must pay option's premium
IV. seller is obligated to fulfill the contract

a. I., II., III., and IV.
b. I., II., and IV.
c. II., III., and IV.
d. II. and IV.

31. Firms intending to sponsor individuals for FINRA registration are required to review all of the following about the applicant EXCEPT:

a. professional background
b. personal background
c. business character
d. educational background

32. Which of the following is considered a common stock "round lot"?

a. 5 shares
b. 1,000 shares
c. 10 shares
d. 100 shares

33. All of the following are considered "insiders" EXCEPT:

a. officer of the company
b. spouse of an officer of the company
c. 5 percent stockholder in the company
d. accountants of the company

34. An investor is both a new customer to the firm and new to the purchase of penny stocks. Which of the following are important to consider prior to proceeding with a purchase of penny stocks with this firm?

I. due to penny stocks trading below $5 per share, the firm does not have to provide a current quote to the customer for the transaction
II. there should be an assessment by the agent as to the suitability of this purchase for this customer
III. the firm is required to disclose only its own commission on the transaction, but not the agent's
IV. a suitability statement must be signed by the customer

a. II. only
b. II. and IV.
c. I., II., III., and IV.
d. II. and III.

35. The NASD Rules of Fair Practice provide governance over:

I. commissions
II. rules of good delivery
III. dispute resolution
IV. member communications with the public

a. I. and IV.
b. IV. only
c. III. and IV.
d. II. and III.

36. Of the following examples of firm communications with the public, which is meant for a targeted audience as opposed to a general audience?

a. Internet postings
b. websites accessible to the public
c. research reports
d. recorded telemarketing messages

37. Investors view warrants as valuable because:

a. the subscription price is always set below the current market price of the common stock
b. they last for up to 10 years
c. they are specifically offered to current shareholders in an effort to provide them preemptive rights
d. all of the above

38. Regarding FINRA member requirements, all of the following are true EXCEPT:

a. pay a fee that is commensurate with the firm's gross income
b. have a minimum of two principals acting to supervise the firm
c. attend an interview for pre-membership
d. all of the above are true

39. Which of the following types of bonds are NOT evidenced by an actual physical certificate?

a. registered bonds
b. bearer bonds
c. book entry bonds
d. principal-only registration

40. Regarding the use of testimonials by firms, which of the following disclosures are they required to make?

I. any third-party contributions in terms of research must include the names of the parties responsible for preparing them
II. the individuals offering their testimony must disclose if they were paid in any way for giving that testimony
III. when referring to the past performance of the firm, statements must be made indicating that any future performance cannot be predicted or guaranteed by past success
IV. if the individual's testimony is given as "an expert," the qualifications that enable this individual to speak as an expert must be provided

a. II., III., and IV.
b. I., II., III., and IV.
c. II. and III.
d. III. and IV.

41. What would be the equivalent dollar price of a corporate bond quoted at 98.75?

a. $98.75
b. $98,750
c. $9.88
d. $987.50

42. A bond's current yield is defined as:

a. the actual interest rate printed on the bond
b. a bond's annual interest relative to its current market price
c. a bond's total annualized return
d. none of the above

43. The announcement of an impending new security offering entering the market is known as:

a. red herring
b. final prospectus
c. tombstone ad
d. none of the above

44. An investor is told that to purchase 1 RYN January 65 call she will be charged an $8 premium. What will be the total cost to this investor to purchase this call?

a. $800
b. $8
c. $80
d. $8,000

45. A warrant that comes attached to a common stock share and provides the investor with the opportunity to purchase an additional common stock share is:

a. an option
b. a right
c. a call
d. a unit

46. Which of the following option positions would be considered by an investor with a "bearish" outlook?

I. selling a call option
II. buying a put option
III. buying a call option
IV. selling a put option

a. III. and IV.
b. I. and II.
c. I. only
d. none of the above

47. Which of the following are TRUE of collateralized mortgage obligations (CMOs)?

I. pay interest and principal annually
II. primary investment risk would be early refinancing
III. divided into tranches that are paid down equally over time, in $1,000 payments
IV. interest rate activity will have little to no effect on them

a. II. only
b. I., II., III., and IV.
c. II. and III.
d. I. and IV.

48. Which of the following activities to be performed by broker-dealer employees necessitates their need to be fingerprinted?

a. preparing records of original entry
b. interacting or having access to securities or cash
c. sale of securities
d. all of these activities require that the employee be fingerprinted

49. Choose the correct notation for a call contract providing the right to purchase 500 shares of KTN at $29 per share, and with an expiration date of May.

a. 500 KTN May 29 call
b. 5 KTN 29 May call
c. 5 KTN May 29 call
d. 5 KTN call May 29

50. Which of the following does NOT influence the determination of an option's premium?

a. overall direction of current market conditions, an upward or downward trend
b. time left until expiration of the contract
c. interest rates
d. volatility levels of the option contract's underlying stock

51. A dividend of $2.25 is declared for security CSU. It will be paid out to all shareholders of record as of Friday, March 12. On the day prior to the ex-dividend date, CSU closed at $54.75. What will be the ex-dividend date, and at what price will the stock open at on that date?

a. Tuesday, March 9, and $54.75
b. Tuesday, March 9, and $52.50
c. Wednesday, March 10, and $54.75
d. Wednesday, March 10, and $52.50

52. Which of the following is TRUE regarding stockholder proxies?

a. brokerage firms may never disclose a shareholder's contact information to a corporation
b. member firms may vote at their own discretion on proxies that are not returned to them by shareholders at least 10 days prior to the annual meeting, given the issue is of less significance
c. member firms are responsible for forwarding proxies to the appropriate beneficial owners, but must do so at their own expense
d. signed proxies with no vote indicated will be voted at the discretion of the member firm

53. An applicant beginning the registration process with a securities firm was concerned about the types of information he would be required to provide on his Form U4. Of the following types of personal information, which is the ONLY one he will be REQUIRED to disclose?

a. a declaration of personal bankruptcy
b. personal net worth
c. marital status
d. educational background

54. Which of the following are valid reasons for a buying firm to reject the delivery of securities purchased from another firm?

I. a "called" bond is delivered and had not been identified as such at the time of the trade
II. delivery is made before the official settlement date
III. associated signatures are not guaranteed
IV. delivery does not contain all associated attachments

a. II. and IV.
b. III. and IV.
c. II. only
d. I., II., III., and IV.

55. Which of the following departments within a brokerage firm is responsible for managing the cash and securities coming into and going out of the firm?

a. sales department
b. cashiering department
c. purchase and sales department
d. custody department

56. Which of the following individuals is/are required to become Series 99 registered?

I. firm employee meeting the definition of "covered person" and works under the "covered" function of handling bank reconciliations
II. firm employee not meeting the definition of "covered person," but works under the "covered" function of preparing financial reports
III. firm employee not meeting the definition of "covered person," but works under the "covered" function of stock lending
IV. firm employee meeting the definition of "covered person" and works under the "covered" function of creating or maintaining general ledgers

a. I. and IV.
b. II. and III.
c. I., II., III., and IV.
d. I. and III.

57. An offering's final prospectus must include all of the following EXCEPT:

a. underwriter's discount
b. issuer's history of being in business
c. description of the underwriting
d. general demographic information regarding all shareholders

58. Which of the following is the date when the buyer of a security officially becomes the owner of record?

a. payment date
b. record date
c. settlement date
d. trade date

59. All of the following would provide for "good delivery" EXCEPT:

a. securities have the signatures of all of the owners, even the one that is recently deceased
b. include a uniform delivery ticket
c. be in the appropriate and correct denominations
d. delivered with all attachments

60. Which of the following is only required to be disclosed by firms to customers at a minimum of every 6 months?

a. account interest received and charged
b. firm's balance sheet
c. account additions of securities
d. all of the above

61. An investment adviser conducts business in Arizona, has no office there, and only does business with financial institutions. He is federally registered and only manages portfolios totaling $200,000,000 or more. Which of the following qualifies him for exemption from state registration as an investment adviser?

a. he conducts business in Arizona but has no established office there
b. he only manages portfolios totaling $200,000,000 or more
c. he is federally registered
d. all of the above

62. An investor purchases securities in an offering and finds that there were false statements made in the prospectus under which those securities were purchased. This investor may seek to obtain financial relief and compensation for the error from any or all of the following EXCEPT:

a. officers of the issuing firm
b. anyone who signed the registration statement
c. all accounting and legal employees responsible for the preparation of the registration statement
d. all of the above may be responsible for providing financial relief to this investor

63. Tombstone ads are:

a. the only advertising authorized for use during the cooling-off period
b. required to be filed with the SEC prior to distribution
c. required for every new issue offering
d. not authorized to include the price of the security

64. The ex-dividend date is:

a. date by which purchasers of a security must have their name officially on a security's stock certificate in order to be entitled to receive a company's declared dividend
b. first date on which purchasers of a security are entitled to receive a company's declared dividend
c. first date on which purchasers of a security are no longer entitled to receive a company's declared dividend
d. date that a dividend is actually paid

65. Which of the following pieces of information will be found in BOTH a preliminary prospectus and a final prospectus?

a. prospective security's price range
b. effective date
c. proceeds going to the issuer
d. all of the above will ONLY be found in the final prospectus, and NOT in the preliminary prospectus

66. Semiannual interest payments on bonds may only be paid in certain months. In which of the following pairs of months can this interest be paid?

a. March and October
b. March and September
c. February and June
d. May and October

67. On the ex-dividend date, a stock's price:

a. will have a reduction made to it that will reflect the amount of the dividend being paid
b. will be increased to reflect the amount of the dividend being paid
c. cannot be determined based only on the information given here
d. will remain the same as prior to the ex-dividend date

68. A Form U4 is used by a firm to collect which of the following pieces of information from new employees as they begin their registration process?

I. their legal name, including previous aliases
II. their employment history for the past eight years
III. their residential history for the past four years
IV. their history of legal or regulatory actions participated in, if any

a. I. and II.
b. I., II., III., and IV.
c. I. and IV.
d. I., III., and IV.

69. Which of the following defines regular-way settlement for corporate stocks and bonds, and municipal bonds?

a. trade date plus three days
b. trade date plus five days
c. next day
d. same day as trade date

70. In reviewing a pool of registration applicants, a firm must consider their abilities in which of the following areas prior to recommending them to proceed with the registration process?

I. experience
II. competence
III. character
IV. training

a. I. and II.
b. I. and IV.
c. I. only
d. I., II., III., and IV.

71. What would be the calculated accrued interest on corporate securities with a principal totaling $5,500, an interest rate of 6 percent, and 73 accrued days?

a. $6,699
b. $263.01
c. $66.99
d. $669.90

72. Blue-sky laws:

a. originated in the Uniform Securities Act and are state based
b. set forth the rules for members of the securities industry regarding their business transactions with other members
c. provide US taxpayers with all information regarding their tax liabilities
d. none of the above

73. Which of the following are required for all customer confirmations?

a. whether the firm makes a market in the security
b. bond yield information
c. CUSIP number
d. all of the above

74. Regarding the termination process of a registered representative, all of the following are true EXCEPT:

a. within 30 days of their termination, the member employee must fill out and submit a Form U5 to FINRA
b. their registration may be transferred to their next place of employment by filling out and submitting a new Form U4 prior to their termination
c. registered representatives who choose to work outside of the industry have up to 24 months to re-enter without having to qualify for re-entry by exam
d. representatives who terminate their employment due to active duty with the military may have their registrations "tolled"

75. A customer fails to make payment on her securities purchase in the required trade date plus five days. Which of the following is TRUE of the consequences of this violation?

I. once the brokerage firm lifts the "freeze" from the delinquent customer's account, the customer will no longer be required to deposit money up front for purchases made, but her account will be limited in other ways for an additional 30-day probationary period
II. on the sixth day following the trade date, the brokerage firm will "sell out" the securities for which payment was not received
III. any loss that may be incurred by the brokerage firm in "selling out" the delinquent customer's securities will be the responsibility of that customer
IV. a "freeze" will be put the customer's account by the firm, which will require an up-front money deposit for any purchases made by the customer for the next 120 days

a. I., II., and III.
b. I., II., III., and IV.
c. II. and IV.
d. II. and III.

76. A customer has a new margin account and purchases 12,000 shares of MNO at a per-share price of $25. If Reg. T dictates a required 50 percent deposit, what would this customer's equity position be?

a. $285,000
b. $15,000
c. $28,500
d. $150,000

77. Which of the following is TRUE of private placements/regulation D offerings?

a. investors are required to hold these securities for at least one year
b. these offerings are limitless in terms of the amount of money that can be raised
c. there is a limited number of accredited investors who may participate in the offering and which varies by the size of the offering
d. sold to accredited investors with a net worth of at least $750,000

78. Which of the following is/are TRUE of a brokerage firm acting in the capacity of the role of a dealer?

I. market maker
II. charges either a markup or markdown for services provided
III. charges a commission for services provided
IV. acts as a principal in trades

a. I., II., and IV.
b. II. and IV.
c. I. only
d. I., III., and IV.

79. An investor buys 12,000 shares of TRE at $8 per share. What is the minimum equity amount this investor is required to maintain on their margin account?

a. $96,000
b. $10,000
c. $24,000
d. $3,000

80. Which of the following is EXEMPT from the requirement to file an underwriting agreement with the corporate finance department?

a. municipal securities
b. private placements
c. US government securities
d. all of the above are exempt from filing an underwriting agreement

81. An investor places an order to sell 300 shares of MFN for $68 per share. MFN declares a 2:1 stock split. What, if any, impact will the split have on this investor's order?

a. sell 600 MFN at 34
b. sell 150 MFN at 136
c. sell 300 MFN at 34
d. sell 300 MFN at 68

82. With regards to a corporate offering, which of the following is the responsibility of the issuer?

I. marketing the offering to investors
II. filing the statement of registration with the SEC
III. blue-skying the issue
IV. contributing to defining the terms of the offering

a. I. and IV.
b. II. and III.
c. II. and IV.
d. II., III., and IV.

83. All of the following are true of a designated market maker (DMM) EXCEPT:

a. all transactions involving the DMM's assigned stock or group of stocks must be executed in front of it
b. DMM is an independent exchange member
c. DMM may only act as a principal in a transaction
d. DMM buys or sells from its own account for the stock or group of stocks it has been assigned

84. An investor has a margin account with both long and short positions. What would be the calculated equity position of this investor's combined account given the following:

long market value (LMV): $84,000
debit: $13,500
short market value (SMV): $23,100
credit: $89,600

a. $131,000
b. $4,000
c. $137,600
d. none of the above

85. An investor would like to purchase shares of company TRE and places an order to buy 350 shares at $55 per share GTC. TRE is to be trading ex-dividend the next day and accordingly would open at $.75 below its previous day's trading price of $57.75. If this investor wants his order to NOT reflect this dividend distribution, what order should he place?

a. buy 350 TRE 55 GTC NDD
b. buy 350 TRE 57 GTC DNR
c. buy 350 TRE 55 GTC
d. buy 350 TRE 55 GTC DNR

86. A customer puts in an order with her brokerage firm to purchase 250 shares of GLP. If this firm currently carries no inventory position in GLP and intends to charge the customer a markup, what type of transaction would the firm execute in order to fill this customer's order?

a. net transaction
b. riskless principal transaction
c. proceeds transaction
d. none of the above

87. Religious and charitable organizations are NOT exempt from which of the following types of provisions from the Securities Act of 1933?

a. antifraud
b. registration
c. prospectus
d. they are exempt of ALL of the above types of provisions

88. In deciding whether a customer is "long a security" with regards to his sell order, firms will ask which of the following as an affirmative determination of the customer in fact being long in his position?

I. has he purchased the security
II. has he submitted instructions to exercise an option for purchase of the shares
III. does he have possession of the security now
IV. has he exercised his right for share conversion from a convertible bond

a. I. and III.
b. III. only
c. I., II., III., and III.
d. I., III., and IV.

89. An investor, who purchased 250 shares of PIX at $52 a share a few months ago, observes that the company's stock is on an upward trend, currently trading at $64 per share. It is widely believed in the market that PIX's earnings report will come in below expectations tomorrow. Fearful of a price drop to her original purchase price of $52, this investor should do which of the following in order to retain the largest profit possible on this purchase transaction?

a. sell 250 at $55 stop
b. sell 250 at $52 stop
c. sell 250 at $56 stop
d. sell 250 at $60 stop

90. A customer purchases 3,000 shares of DSY at a per-share price of $12 and a total long market value (LMV) of $36,000. What would this customer's equity and excess equity be on this position, given that Reg. T is at 50 percent and the per-share price increases from $12 to $19 per share?

a. $57,000, $28,500
b. $39,000, $10,500
c. $18,000, $10,500
d. none of the above

91. Rule 145 covers:

I. changes in par value
II. reverse splits
III. stock splits
IV. reclassification of company securities as the result of an exchange of one class for another

a. I., II., III., and IV.
b. II. and III.
c. IV. only
d. II., III., and IV.

92. Of the following types of orders, which type CANNOT be accepted by a specialist/DMM?

a. GTC orders
b. FOK orders
c. stop orders
d. all of the above may be accepted by the specialist/DMM

93. Private-placement purchased stock is known as:

a. legend stock
b. restricted stock
c. lettered stock
d. all of the above

94. The review by FINRA of underwriting agreements entails all of the following EXCEPT:

a. if not filed with the SEC, deadline for submission for review is within 15 days of the expected offering date
b. deadline for submission to FINRA for review is one day after the SEC registration filing
c. submission of the agreement must include the minimum offering price
d. there will be a "fair and reasonable" review of the underwriter's maximum compensation with regards to the specific offering

95. Two orders in for trade execution are for the same price. Which of the following are considered in determining the sequence of how the orders will be filled?

I. parity
II. priority
III. profit
IV. precedence

a. I., II., and IV.
b. II. only
c. II. and III. only
d. I. and IV.

96. All of the following are true of NASDAQ trades EXCEPT:

a. negotiations are accomplished via workstations or over the phone
b. prices on securities are negotiated directly between broker-dealers
c. any ongoing negotiations within this interdealer network are kept private between the two parties
d. trades are done between the hours of 9:00 a.m. and 4:00 p.m. EST.

97. A review of an underwriting agreement includes determining which expenses are to be considered underwriter's compensation and which aren't. Of the following, which expense WOULD be considered a type of compensation?

a. blue-sky fees incurred
b. finders' fee that the issuer will be reimbursing
c. accounting-related fees
d. any printing costs

98. A US-based issuer would like to make an offering of securities only to investors outside of the United States, and would specifically restrict any securities from being offered for sale within the US Which of the following would this investor utilize to do that?

a. Regulation S offering
b. Rule 147 offering
c. Regulation A offering
d. Regulation D offering

99. Of the following types of orders used to purchase and sell securities, which allows for an investor to set a maximum price for which he is willing to pay for a security?

a. buy stop order
b. buy limit order
c. sell limit order
d. market order

100. Which of the following would be considered a "qualified institutional buyer" (QIB) for the purposes of the resale of restricted stock and Rule 144a?

a. trust fund with investments totaling $22,000,000
b. insurance company with investments totaling $96,000,000
c. pension plan with investments totaling $102,000,000
d. investment company with investments totaling $44,000,000

Answer Key and Explanations

1. C: Given that par value of preferred stock shares is $100:

$$\$100 \text{ par value } \times \text{dividend percent} = \text{per share annual income}$$

$$\$100 \times .07 = \$7 \text{ per share}$$

$$\text{per share annual income } \times \# \text{ or preferred shares owned } = \text{total annual income}$$

$$\$7 \times 75 = \$525$$

2. A: During the distribution of a stock dividend, the stock price of individual shares will DECREASE, not increase, in order to reflect the additional outstanding shares that now exist in the market. A stock dividend is utilized by a company that would like to reward their shareholders without consuming cash. Investors receive a number of additional shares based on the number currently owned prior to the dividend, and the overall market value of the stock remains unchanged after the dividend distribution.

3. D: A corporation would be motivated to repurchase its own shares as a means to fund an acquisition, retain control over the company, or increase the company's earnings per share.

4. A:

$$\text{annual income} = \text{quarterly dividend} \times 4$$

$$\$1.50 \times 4 = \$6.00$$

$$\text{current yield} = \frac{\text{annual income}}{\text{current market price}}$$

$$\text{current yield} = \frac{\$6.00}{\$32.50} = .1846 = 18.5 \text{ percent}$$

5. C:

$$\# \text{ of shares after conversion} = \frac{\text{par value}}{\text{conversion price}}$$

$$\frac{\$100}{\$5} = 20 \text{ shares of DSY common stock}$$

6. B: The book value of a corporation is calculated by subtracting, NOT adding, all of its liabilities from its total assets. Additionally, it's true that dividing the total book value of a company by the number of outstanding shares will result in a per-share book value, and book value can be defined as a company's liquidation value.

7. D: Stockholders are NOT afforded the right to have access to any of the company's confidential financial information. They are, however, afforded the right to a claim on residual assets post-bankruptcy, to inspect the company's books and records, and to receive a list of the company's shareholders.

8. C:

$$\text{\# of shares to be received} = \text{\# of shares owned} \times \text{percent dividend payout}$$

$$1{,}500 \times 3 \text{ percent} = 1{,}500 \times .03 = 45 \text{ shares}$$

9. B: Preferred stock is often nonvoting, but shareholders may be provided with the right to vote in the event that several dividend payments have been missed by the company. Preferred stock has no maturity date, is sensitive to interest rates, and provides for a priority claim over common stockholders for dividend distribution.

10. C: Equity represents ownership in the company that issues it and provides a means for a corporation to raise capital. At the point of maturity, DEBT, not equity, will allow for an investor to receive his investment amount back. Additionally, debt instruments, not equity, create a creditor relationship between those who invest and the corporation of issuance.

11. D: The call feature is designed to benefit the company, NOT the investor. By calling back preferred shares, the company may be either eliminating its obligation to pay a fixed dividend payment altogether, or benefitting from a reduced rate of dividend payment on newly issued shares that have a lower rate than those previously sold. Callable preferred shares may be called during a rate decline in order to then sell new preferred shares with a lower fixed dividend rate. They are most often called at a premium to par, and their call protection provides for some delay past issuance in which the shares cannot be called by the company.

12. B:

$$\text{per share profit} = \text{current market share price} - \text{purchase share price}$$

$$\$74.50 - \$55.50 = \$19.00 \text{ per share profit}$$

$$\text{total profit} = \text{per share profit} \times \text{\# of shares sold}$$

$$\$19.00 \times 250 = \$4{,}750.00 \text{ total profit}$$

13. D: A company is obligated to pay dividends to its preferred stockholders. Additionally, preferred stock represents ownership in the company and provides for payment of semiannual dividends that are set at a fixed rate.

14. A: Stock that has been sold to investors and then purchased back by the issuing corporation is known as treasury stock. Outstanding stock is sold stock that still remains with investors. Authorized stock is the largest amount of stock that an issuing corporation may sell to investors. Issued stock is the authorized stock that has actually been sold to investors.

15. C: A shareholder's preemptive right in a rights offering may be sold to another investor interested in buying the newly offered shares, or exercised by submitting payment and the rights in return for the shares. The rights afford the stockholder the opportunity to purchase the newly offered shares at a discount; however, the subscription price remains fixed for 45 days, NOT 35.

16. B: All of the above can be considered securities EXCEPT the fixed annuity. In order for an investment product to be considered a security, it must be transferable AND the owner of it must take on the risk of loss of some portion or all of her invested amount. Bonds, mutual funds, and variable annuities all meet those requirements. A fixed annuity is an insurance contract that provides for GUARANTEED fixed payments and thus presents no risk to the investor regarding any loss of his investment.

17. C: Given that par value of preferred stock shares is $100:

$$\$100 \text{ par value } \times \text{dividend percent} = \text{per share annual income}$$

$$\$100 \times .06 = \$6 \text{ per share}$$

$$\text{per share annual income } \times \# \text{ of preferred shares owned} = \text{total annual income}$$

$$\$6 \times 100 = \$600$$

The company is in arrears for the current year plus two, so the total years in arrears is three. Therefore:

$$3 \times \$600 = \$1{,}800$$

The company owes this investor $1,800 in accumulated unpaid dividends for the current year, plus two.

18. A: Given that this investor owns 650 shares of PPG and there are two board members to be elected, the number of votes she is allowed to cast is as follows:

$$\text{total votes to cast} = \# \text{ of owned shares } \times \# \text{ of individuals to be elected}$$

$$650 \times 2 = 1{,}300 \text{ votes}$$

The statutory method of voting involves having the voter cast an equal number of votes for each of the candidates she would like to vote for. With two candidates to be elected, this investor would split her 1,300 votes and cast them in an equal amount of 650 for each candidate.

19. D: An option seller receives his income from the premium paid to him by the buyer of the option. Further, he is obligated under the terms of the option contract to perform, given the buyer chooses to exercise her rights under the contract. An option seller will NOT want the option to be exercised and instead would prefer it expire unexercised, so as to not be obligated to perform under the contract AND to profit simply from the premium income he received. Accordingly, upon expiration of the contract, the seller does NOT lose money and in fact that is where his income is made.

20. C: Mediation is the type of dispute resolution that does NOT always end in a final binding decision regarding the issue being disputed. The mediation process can produce one of three possible outcomes: an agreement between the parties may result; either the mediator or one of the parties withdraws from the process; or the mediator sees no potential for resolution and declares an impasse. Given that, the potential for no binding decision being reached at the end of the mediation process is entirely possible. Simplified arbitration is for disputes involving $50,000 or less and concludes with a decision handed down by an arbitrator. Arbitration for disputes of a larger amount is submitted to a panel of arbitrators who then provide a decision on the matter. In a minor rules violation (MRV) procedure, the outcome can be censure, a fine of $2,500, or a formal hearing resulting in a variety of potential penalties being imposed.

21. A: The Securities Investor Protection Corporation (SIPC) was established for the protection of customers. SIPC will petition for the appointment of a trustee to liquidate a firm should it fail to meet its minimum capital requirement. Further, broker-dealer membership with SIPC is required if registered with the SEC. Upon having a trustee appointed for the purpose of liquidation, SIPC will require the firm to NOT conduct any business at all, and SIPC is a government-sponsored corporation, NOT a private corporation.

22. B: MSRB Rule G-38 limits a municipal finance professional (MFP) to making donations of $250 or less (per candidate, per election) and only to candidates who are participating in elections that they themselves are eligible to vote in. Here a violation occurred due to the donation being for more than $250, and for an election the MFP is not eligible to vote in. The penalty for such a violation is the MFP's firm being prohibited from participating in the business of municipal securities for that issuer for two years, NOT one.

23. B: Due to institutional investors tending to be larger in size and higher in their level of sophistication, FEWER, not more, laws are in place for their protection. Institutional accounts do, however, have no minimum size requirements, institutional investors must maintain their communications for three years, and government agencies are considered to be institutional investors.

24. C: Regulation T regulates broker-dealers in their extension of credit for the purchase of securities. Banks (for the same purpose) are regulated by Regulation U, and similarly, all other financial institutions are regulated by Regulation G.

25. D: If the offer of a minor rules violation procedure resolution is accepted by the FINRA member under review, the maximum penalty to be imposed if a violation is found is a censure and a $2,500 fine. If, however, the offer to proceed with a minor rules violation procedure is NOT accepted and a "formal" hearing by the Department of Enforcement becomes necessary, one of the several penalties that can be imposed is a fine in whatever amount the department finds appropriate. Other penalties are a suspension of up to one year and an expulsion for up to 10 years.

26. A: Retail communications are made to be accessible to 25 retail investors or more, but over a 30-day period of time, NOT 60. Further, retail communications include sales literature, must be maintained by the member firm for three years, and can be distributed electronically or by hard copy.

27. B: Credit risk is defined as the risk that the issuer of the bonds will not be able to fulfill its financial obligations under the terms of the bond. Given that, the US government is the debt issuer here that carries the least amount of credit risk. Just behind in terms of risk would be US government agencies, followed by municipal bonds, and then corporate bonds.

28. D: SIPC firm coverage in the event of broker-dealer failure covers up to a total of $500,000 per separate customer, $250,000 of which can be in the form of cash. Given that, the account totaling $490,000, with $325,000 in securities and $165,000 in cash, will be the one fully covered by SIPC. The other account choices all either have combined securities and cash totals that are over $500,000 OR a cash total that exceeds the $250,000 coverage maximum.

29. A: "Established customer" status within a firm for the purposes of exemption from the penny stock cold call rule would involve the customer executing three separate transactions over three different days, involving three different penny stocks.

30. C: An option contract provides a buyer, upon payment of the option premium to the seller, the right to buy or sell a security. Because of the premium paid, the buyer is NOT obligated to perform under the contract. The seller, upon entering into the contract and taking receipt of the premium, IS obligated to fulfill the contract as stated if the buyer chooses to perform.

31. B: Firms intending to sponsor individuals for FINRA registration are required to review an applicant's professional background, business character, and educational background. They are NOT required to look into an applicant's personal background or history.

32. D: A round lot for either common or preferred stock is 100 shares. For bonds, a round lot is considered to be five shares.

33. C: "Insiders" can be officers of the company, or any spouse of an officer of the company. Further, "insiders" may be any stockholders with 10 percent stake in the company or greater, NOT 5 percent.

34. B: Prior to proceeding with a purchase of penny stocks, this investor should consider that her agent will be making an assessment of suitability for her with regard to this purchase, and that she will need to sign a suitability statement regarding the transaction. Further, the firm WILL be required to provide a current quote of the stock regardless of its price, and the firm is also required to disclose BOTH its own commission as well as the agent's commission on the transaction.

35. A: The NASD Rules of Fair Practice provide governance over member interactions with the public. Accordingly, two of the topics that fall under these rules are those regarding member commissions and member communications with the public. Rules of good delivery fall under the Uniform Practice Code that oversees FINRA members and their dealings with one another. Dispute resolution comes from the Code of Arbitration and pertains to disputes that occur between members and other members, registered agents, customers, and banks.

36. C: Firms create research reports that are written for a specific audience with specific interests, distributed to a limited group, and therefore qualify as meant for a targeted audience. Internet postings, websites accessible to the public, and recorded telemarketing messages are produced for the general public, and are made accessible to the general public.

37. B: Investment value for warrants comes from their extended life, which is much longer than rights provide and can last up to 10 years. The investor may have up to that long to buy stock at the offered subscription price. The subscription price of warrants is always set ABOVE, not below, current market value, and rights are offered to current shareholders in an effort to provide them preemptive rights, NOT warrants.

38. D: FINRA member requirements state that, among other things, members must pay a fee that is commensurate with the firm's gross income, have a minimum of two principals acting to supervise the firm, and attend an interview for pre-membership.

39. C: Book entry bonds are NOT evidenced by an actual physical certificate and instead provide the investor with proof of ownership through their trade confirmation. Registered bonds, bearer bonds, and principal-only registration bonds all provide for a physical certificate.

40. B: Firms that utilize testimonials are required to include the names of any third-party contributors of research, if used. Individuals, if compensated, must disclose that they were. When referring to the firm's past performance, statements must be made indicating that any future performance cannot be predicted or guaranteed by past success. If providing "expert" testimony, individuals should disclose any qualifications that support that they are in fact experts qualified to give such opinions.

41. D: Corporate bonds are priced as a percentage of par, par value being $1,000.

$$\text{percent of par} \times \$1{,}000 = \text{bond price}$$

$$98.75 = 98.75 \text{ percent}$$

$$98.75 \text{ percent} \times \$1{,}000 = .9875 \times \$1{,}000 = \$987.50$$

42. B: A bond's current yield is its annual interest relative to its current market price, and is calculated as:

$$\text{annual income} / \text{current market price}$$

The actual interest rate printed on a bond is called its nominal yield, and a bond's total annualized return is its yield to maturity.

43. C: A tombstone ad is simply an announcement of an impending new security offering entering the market; it contains only the most basic of information, and makes no offers of sales. A red herring, also known as a preliminary prospectus, contains information that is not final, and is used primarily to cultivate interest for the offering. The final prospectus contains the final offering price and stands as the official offer of sale to potential investors along with all of the required and necessary information needed to make the decision to purchase.

44. A: Option contracts are sold in round lots of 100 shares each. Here the contract is for 1 round lot, or 100 shares.

$$\text{total cost of call} = \text{premium} \times \text{contracted \# of shares in call}$$

$$\$8 \times 100 = \$800$$

45. D: A warrant that comes attached to a common stock share and provides the investor with the opportunity to purchase an additional common stock share is a unit. An option involves two investors contracting to buy or sell a security at an agreed-upon price, with the contract lasting the duration of a specific period of time. A right is offered to existing shareholders in order to provide for their preemptive right to purchase additional shares in the event that the company sells shares in a new offering. A call is an option to purchase a specific amount of an underlying security, for the duration of a specific period of time, and for a fixed and agreed-upon price.

46. B: An investor with a "bearish" outlook on a stock is one who believes the stock's price will fall. Given that, he would want to participate in option positions that would benefit from that price drop.

Selling a call option to an investor to buy shares below their current market price would benefit from a price drop in that the buyer of the option will only exercise her option given a price increase. If the seller believes the share price will be declining, he will sell the call option in hopes that the call will expire without being exercised and he will profit from the premium paid to him by the buyer of the option.

Buying a put option to sell shares above their current market price would benefit from a price drop in that the investor could buy the shares low (once the share price has dropped) and profit from the then-contracted sale at a price above the purchase price. The gain is the sale price minus the purchase price.

47. A: Collateralized mortgage obligations (CMOs) have early refinancing as their primary investment risk. They pay interest and principal monthly, NOT annually. They are structured investments, divided into tranches of differing maturity schedules that pay principal to ONLY one tranche at a time in $1,000 payments. Interest rate activity will have a significant effect on CMOs in that a rise or fall in rates will determine the rate at which homeowners will refinance (faster or slower) and, accordingly, the rate at which investors of CMOs will be paid off.

48. D: A broker-dealer employee who prepares records of original entry, interacts or has access to securities or cash, or participates in the sale of securities should be required to be fingerprinted.

49. C: Option contracts are sold in round lots of 100 shares each. To correctly note this contract, first should come the number of shares in round lots of 100, here 5. Next is the stock symbol, KTN, the contract expiration date, May, the per-share price for the contract, $29, and, finally, the specification of being a "call" contract.

50. A: The overall direction of current market conditions, meaning an upward or downward trend, will NOT directly influence the determination of an option's premium. The time left until the expiration of the contract, interest rates, and the volatility levels of the option contract's underlying stock WILL influence the determination of the contract's option premium.

51. D: Given the dividend is declared for any shareholder of record as of Friday, March 12, the ex-dividend date would be Wednesday, March 10, or two business days prior to the record date. The stock price for CSU will then be reduced by $2.25 for any purchases made as of the ex-dividend date in order to account for the declared dividend amount that those shareholders will not be entitled to receive.

$$\$54.75 - \$2.25 = \$52.50$$

The stock price for CSU at its opening on Wednesday, March 10, would be $52.50.

52. B: It is TRUE that member firms may vote at their own discretion on proxies that are not returned to them by shareholders at least 10 days prior to the annual meeting, given the issue is of less significance. They do NOT, however, have the authority to vote at their discretion if the issue is of major significance.

Brokerage firms MAY disclose a shareholder's contact information to a corporation as long as they have been given the authority to do so by the shareholder. Member firms are responsible for forwarding proxies to the appropriate beneficial owners, and should be reimbursed for any reasonable expenses incurred by doing so. Signed proxies with no vote indicated will NOT be voted at the discretion of their member firm, but instead will be voted in accordance with the issuer's preference.

53. A: This applicant will be required to disclose whether he's declared bankruptcy, but will NOT be required to provide information regarding his personal net worth, marital status, or educational background.

54. D: Valid reasons for a buying firm to reject delivery of securities purchased from another firm are a "called" bond is delivered and was not identified as such at the time of the trade, delivery was made before the official settlement date, the associated signatures are not guaranteed, and delivery does not contain all of the associated attachments.

55. B: The department responsible for managing the cash and securities coming into and going out of a securities firm is the cashiering department. The sales department is where investors and registered representatives interact within the market with recommendations being made and orders being placed. The purchase and sales department handle the input of transactions into customer accounts, as well as billing. The custody department has possession of the physical securities of both the firm and its customers.

56. A: In order for a firm employee to be required to become Series 99 registered, she must BOTH meet the definition of a "covered person" AND within her role perform a "covered function." Accordingly, here the two employees who meet the definition of "covered persons" and perform the "covered" functions of handling bank reconciliations and creating or maintaining general ledgers, would be required to become Series 99 registered. The employees performing the "covered" functions of preparing financial reports and stock lending would NOT be required to become Series 99 registered, given that they both do NOT meet the definition of "covered person" within their roles in the firm.

57. D: An offering's final prospectus must NOT include general demographic information regarding ALL shareholders, but instead must include only information regarding the larger shareholders. Conversely, the final prospectus MUST include the underwriter's discount, the issuer's history of being in business, and a description of the underwriting.

58. C: The settlement date is the date when the buyer of a security officially becomes the owner of record. The payment date is the date by which a buyer of a security has to have his payment for his purchase to the brokerage firm. The record date is the date that decides which shareholders will be entitled to receive a declared dividend from the corporation. The trade date is the actual date of execution for the market order.

59. A: "Good delivery" would require that the securities have all of the signatures of the owners of record; however, all owners must be alive. Further, the securities must include a uniform delivery ticket, be in the appropriate and correct denominations, and be delivered with all attachments.

60. B: Firms are REQUIRED to disclose to their customers their balance sheet every six months. The account interest received and charged, and any additions of securities, must be disclosed at least quarterly assuming inactivity in the account, and monthly for months when activity occurs.

61. D: Investment advisers must meet certain conditions in order to conduct securities business without state registration. This investment adviser qualifies for an exemption from state registration due to being federally registered; conducting business within Arizona only with financial institutions and without having an established office there; and only managing portfolios totaling $200,000,000 or more.

62. C: This investor who purchases securities under an offering where false statements were made in the offering's prospectus is entitled to seek financial relief from certain responsible individuals. She may NOT, however, seek relief from ALL accounting and legal employees responsible for the preparation of the registration statement. She may instead seek financial relief from the accountants and attorneys who actually prepared the registration statement. Further, she may seek financial relief from the officers of the issuing firm and anyone who signed the registration statement.

63. A: Tombstone ads are the only advertising authorized for use during the cooling-off period. They do NOT need to be filed with the SEC prior to distribution, are NOT required for every new issue offering, and ARE authorized to include the price of the security.

64. C: The ex-dividend date is the first date on which purchasers of a security are no longer entitled to receive a company's declared dividend. At this point, the stock would be traded WITHOUT the dividend attached. The date by which purchasers of a security must have their name officially on a security's stock certificate in order to be entitled to receive a company's declared dividend is the record date. The declaration date is the day when a company's board of directors decides to pay a dividend and, accordingly, the date on which all stockholders of record are entitled to receive a company's declared dividend. The date that a dividend is actually paid is the payment date.

65. A: A security's price range for an offering will be found in BOTH a preliminary prospectus and a final prospectus. The preliminary prospectus will have the price range of the offering and the final prospectus will have the actual offering price.

The effective date and the proceeds going to the issuer will ONLY be found in the final prospectus.

66. B: Semiannual interest payments on bonds may only be paid in certain months and only on the first or the fifteenth day of the month. Of the pairs of months given here, the months when this interest may be paid are March and September, which then qualifies the payment as semiannual and, accordingly, every six months.

67. A: On the ex-dividend date, a stock's price will have a reduction made to it that will reflect the amount of the dividend being paid. This due to any new purchasers from that date forward not being entitled to receive that dividend.

68. C: A Form U4 is used by a firm to collect a new employee's legal name, including aliases, and history of any legal or regulatory actions he's participated in, if any. The Form U4 also collects his employment history, but for 10 years, not eight, and his residential history for five years, not four.

69. A: Regular-way settlement for corporate stocks and bonds, and municipal bonds, is the trade date plus three days. The trade date plus five days is the payment date, NOT the settlement date, for securities. Next-day settlement is reserved for trades where both the cash payment and securities are available for delivery on the next business day, and same-day settlement is for those with cash and securities available the same day as the trade.

70. D: In reviewing a pool of registration applicants, a firm must consider their individual levels of experience, competence, character, and training prior to recommending them to proceed with the registration process

71. C:

$$\text{accrued interest} = (\text{principal} \times \text{interest rate}) \times \left(\frac{\text{\# of days}}{360}\right)$$

$$(\$5{,}500 \times .06) \times \left(\frac{73}{360}\right) = \$330 \times .203 = \$66.99$$

72. A: Blue-sky laws originated in the Uniform Securities Act and are state based. The Uniform Practice Code sets forth the rules for members of the securities industry regarding their business transactions with other members. The Internal Revenue Code provides US taxpayers with information regarding their tax liabilities.

73. D: Customer confirmations, if applicable, must contain whether the firm makes a market in the security, the bond yield information, and CUSIP number.

74. B: A registered representative's registration may NOT be transferred to her next place of employment. Prior to leaving, she must submit a Form U5 terminating her registration with her current employer and then proceed to begin a new registration process with her new employer.

It is true, however, that within 30 days of her termination, the member employee must fill out and submit a Form U5 to FINRA.

Registered representatives who choose to work outside of the industry have up to 24 months to re-enter without having to qualify for re-entry by exam; however, representatives who terminate their employment due to active duty with the military may have their registrations "tolled" or placed on inactive status, bypassing the 24-month requirement.

75. D: If a customer fails to make payment on her securities purchase in the required trade date plus five days, the brokerage firm on the sixth day will "sell out" the securities for which payment was not received, and any loss that may be incurred by the brokerage firm will be the responsibility of that customer. Once the brokerage firm lifts the "freeze" on the delinquent customer's account, the customer will no longer be required to deposit money up front for purchases made and her account will resume its regular status with the firm, with no further penalties imposed. Finally, the "freeze" placed on the customer's account requiring up-front money deposited for any purchases made by the customer is for the duration of the next 90 days, NOT 120.

76. D:

$$\text{long market value} = \#\text{ of shares } \times \text{ per share price}$$

$$\text{long market value} = 12{,}000 \times \$25 = \$300{,}000$$

$$\text{debit} = \text{long market value } \times \text{ required deposit percent}$$

$$\text{debit} = \$300{,}000 \times .50 = \$150{,}000$$

$$\text{equity} = \text{long market value} - \text{debit}$$

$$\text{equity} = \$300{,}000 - \$150{,}000 = \$150{,}000$$

77. B: Private placement/regulation D offerings are limitless in terms of the amount money that can be raised. Investors are required to hold these securities for at least six months, NOT one year. There is NO limit on the number of accredited investors who may participate in the offering, and the securities are sold to accredited investors with a net worth of at least $1,000,000 (outside of their primary residence), NOT $750,000.

78. A: A brokerage firm acting in the capacity of the role of a dealer will be a market maker, will charge either a markup or markdown for services provided, and will act as a principal in trades. It will NOT, however, charge a commission for services provided, as would be done by a broker.

79. C: On margin accounts, customers must maintain a minimum equity amount that is 25 percent of the account's long market value.

$$\text{minimum equity} = \text{long market value} \times 25 \text{ percent}$$

$$\text{long market value} = \#\text{ of shares} \times \text{per share price}$$

$$\text{long market value} = 12{,}000 \times \$8 = \$96{,}000$$

$$\text{minimum equity} = \$96{,}000 \times .25 = \$24{,}000$$

80. D: Municipal securities, private placements, and US government securities are ALL exempt from the requirement to file an underwriting agreement with the corporate finance department.

81. A: An open order to buy or sell stock for a company for which a forward stock split is declared must be adjusted to reflect that split prior to being executed. The overall value of the order, however, must be the same after the adjustment as it was before.

Here, the number of shares must be multiplied by the fraction of the split 2/1.

$$300 \text{ shares} \times \frac{2}{1} = 600 \text{ shares}$$

The share price must then be multiplied by the reciprocal of the fraction of the split 2/1.

$$\$68 \times \frac{1}{2} = \$34 \text{ per share}$$

The newly calculated order to reflect MFN's 2:1 stock split would be selling 600 MFN at 34.

82. B: For corporate offerings, the issuer's responsibilities include filing the statement of registration with the SEC and blue-skying the issue, which involves registering the securities in any state in which they will be sold. It is the underwriter's responsibility to market the offering to investors and to contribute to defining the terms of the offering.

83. C: A DMM may act as BOTH the principal in a transaction, buying and selling from its own account, and as an agent, executing public orders for a service fee.

Further, the DMM is an independent exchange member. It may buy or sell from its own account for the stock or group of stocks it has been assigned, and all transactions involving the DMM's assigned stock or group of stocks must be executed in front of it.

84. D: A margin account with both long and short positions is called a combined account. The equity on that type of account is calculated as follows:

$$\text{combined account equity} = (\text{LMV} - \text{debit}) + (\text{credit} - \text{SMV})$$

$$\text{combined account equity} = (\$84{,}000 - \$13{,}500) + (\$89{,}600 - \$23{,}100) = \$70{,}500 + \$66{,}500 = \$137{,}000$$

85. D: In order for this investor to specifically request that his order NOT be reduced to reflect TRE's dividend distribution, he must enter the order accordingly as buy 350 TRE 55 GTC DNR. The order will be to buy 350 shares of TRE for $55 per share, with the order to remain "good till cancelled," and the "DNR" to specify his request for no reduction to be made.

86. B: If a firm receives an order for 250 shares of GLP and currently carries no position in GLP, it would proceed with a riskless principal transaction in order to fill the order. It basically takes a position in GLP simply to fill the order and accordingly takes on no risk. The markup charged by the firm will be derived from the actual cost incurred by the dealer.

A net transaction involves the broker-dealer filling the customer's order by buying the security at one price and then selling it to the customer at a higher price. It is this profit that the broker-dealer retains rather than charging a markup on the transaction to the customer.

A proceeds transaction has a broker-dealer handling first a sell order for a customer and then proceeding with the profit from that sale to cover a separate buy order of another security for the customer on the same day. There is a cap of 5 percent to be charged to the customer for the two transactions combined.

87. A: Religious and charitable organizations are NOT exempt from the antifraud provisions from the Securities Act of 1933. They ARE exempt from the registration and prospectus provisions.

88. C: Firms are REQUIRED to establish "affirmative determination" on all customer sell orders in order to validate whether the customer is long the security being sold or whether the customer is selling short and thus must borrow the security in order to satisfy delivery. In establishing affirmative determination, a firm will ask whether the customer has purchased the security, whether the customer has submitted instructions to exercise an option for purchase of the shares, whether the customer has possession of the security now, and whether the customer has exercised his or her right for share conversion from a convertible bond. Any of these circumstances answered in the affirmative will qualify the customer as being "long the security."

89. D: This investor should place an order to sell 250 at $60 stop. In the event that PIX's earnings report does come in below expectations and the share price begins to drop past $60 per share, the order to sell 250 shares will be triggered. It will now become a market order and the shares will be sold at the next available price. The result will be the profit that exists between the original purchase price of $52 per share and whatever price this sell stop order provides.

The same sell stop orders for $56, $55, and $52 would NOT provide as much profit protection for this investor, given that the trigger points for those orders would be lower and the likelihood of their shares being sold at an even lower price would be great.

90. B: ORIGINAL position:

$$\text{long market value (LMV)} = \$36{,}000$$

$$\text{debit} = \text{long market value} \times \text{required deposit percent}$$

$$\text{debit} = \$36{,}000 \times .50 = \$18{,}000$$

$$\text{equity} = \text{long market value} - \text{debit}$$

$$\text{equity} = \$36{,}000 - \$18{,}000 = \$18{,}000$$

NEW position, after share price increase:

$$\text{long market value} = \text{\# of shares} \times \text{per share price}$$

$$\text{long market value} = 3{,}000 \times \$19 = \$57{,}000$$

$$\text{debit} = \$18{,}000$$

$$\text{equity} = \text{long market value} - \text{debit}$$

$$\text{equity} = \$57{,}000 - \$18{,}000 = \$39{,}000$$

$$\text{Reg. T} = \text{long market value (LMV)} \times \text{percent required for deposit}$$

$$\text{Reg. T} = \$57{,}000 \times .50 = \$28{,}500$$

$$\text{excess equity} = \text{equity} - \text{Reg. T required deposit}$$

$$\text{excess equity} = \$39{,}000 - \$28{,}500 = \$10{,}500$$

91. C: Rule 145 provides for shareholder approval of company mergers or reorganizations. Here it covers the reclassification of company securities that result from of an exchange of one class of company securities for another. It does NOT cover changes in par value, reverse splits, and stock splits.

92. B: Specialists/DMMs may NOT accept FOK (fill or kill) orders. These are orders that must be executed in their entirety immediately, or if not, cancelled. Specialists/DMMs MAY accept both GTC (good till cancelled) orders and stop orders.

93. D: Stock purchased through a private placement may be referred to as legend stock, restricted stock, and lettered stock.

94. C: The submission of an offering's underwriting agreement to FINRA must include the MAXIMUM offering price, NOT the minimum. The deadline for submission to FINRA for review is one day after SEC registration filing, and if not filed with the SEC, the deadline is within 15 days of the expected offering date. Further, FINRA in its review will conduct a "fair and reasonable" review of the underwriter's maximum compensation with regard to the specific offering.

95. A: Given two orders in for trade execution coming in at the same price, the sequence of how the orders will be filled is determined by parity, priority, or precedence. Parity is considered when both orders come in with identical time of receipt, price, and size, and result in the available shares being divided between the orders. Priority considers which was received first, with the first order being filled first, and precedence favors the larger of the two orders when their time received and price are the same. Profit is NOT a consideration in determining the sequence of how the orders will be filled.

96. D: NASDAQ trades are accomplished between the hours of 9:30 a.m. and 4:00 p.m. EST, NOT 9:00 a.m. and 4:00 p.m. EST. Negotiations on these trades are accomplished via workstations or over the phone, prices on securities are negotiated directly between broker-dealers, and the ongoing negotiations within this interdealer network are kept private between the two parties.

97. B: In reviewing an underwriting agreement, a finders' fee that the issuer will be reimbursing would be considered underwriter's compensation. Blue-sky fees, accounting-related fees, and any printing costs would NOT be considered underwriter's compensation for the purposes of this review.

98. A: A US-based issuer that would like to make an offering of securities only to investors outside of the United States would participate in a Regulation S offering. By offering sale of these securities ONLY to investors outside of the US, this issuer will qualify for an exemption from filing a registration statement for any securities under the Securities Act of 1933.

A Rule 147 offering involves the sale of securities in only ONE state. A Regulation A offering's primary feature provides for an issuer to raise in any period of 12 months a maximum of $5,000,000. A Regulation D offering is a private placement that is exempt from registration under the Securities Act of 1933 and provides sale to an unlimited number of accredited investors.

99. B: Buy limit orders allow for an investor to set a maximum price for which he is willing to pay for a security. It provides that the investor will NEVER pay more than a specific price for a security, but does not guarantee that the order will be executed.

A buy stop order is used to protect against profit or loss involving a short sale of stock. A sell limit order allows for an investor to set the minimum price he will take for a security. A market order guarantees execution of an order as soon as it's presented to the market, but does NOT guarantee the price of execution.

100. C: A "qualified institutional buyer" (QIB), for the purposes of the resale of restricted stock and Rule 144a, is defined as a company with a minimum of $100,000,000 in investments and can include many types of organizations such as partnerships, banks, trust funds, insurance companies, and investment companies. Here the pension plan with investments totaling $102,000,000 would be considered a QIB for the purposes of Rule 144a. The other three each have investments that individually total less than the $100,000,000 minimum.

How to Overcome Test Anxiety

Just the thought of taking a test is enough to make most people a little nervous. A test is an important event that can have a long-term impact on your future, so it's important to take it seriously and it's natural to feel anxious about performing well. But just because anxiety is normal, that doesn't mean that it's helpful in test taking, or that you should simply accept it as part of your life. Anxiety can have a variety of effects. These effects can be mild, like making you feel slightly nervous, or severe, like blocking your ability to focus or remember even a simple detail.

If you experience test anxiety—whether severe or mild—it's important to know how to beat it. To discover this, first you need to understand what causes test anxiety.

Causes of Test Anxiety

While we often think of anxiety as an uncontrollable emotional state, it can actually be caused by simple, practical things. One of the most common causes of test anxiety is that a person does not feel adequately prepared for their test. This feeling can be the result of many different issues such as poor study habits or lack of organization, but the most common culprit is time management. Starting to study too late, failing to organize your study time to cover all of the material, or being distracted while you study will mean that you're not well prepared for the test. This may lead to cramming the night before, which will cause you to be physically and mentally exhausted for the test. Poor time management also contributes to feelings of stress, fear, and hopelessness as you realize you are not well prepared but don't know what to do about it.

Other times, test anxiety is not related to your preparation for the test but comes from unresolved fear. This may be a past failure on a test, or poor performance on tests in general. It may come from comparing yourself to others who seem to be performing better or from the stress of living up to expectations. Anxiety may be driven by fears of the future—how failure on this test would affect your educational and career goals. These fears are often completely irrational, but they can still negatively impact your test performance.

Elements of Test Anxiety

As mentioned earlier, test anxiety is considered to be an emotional state, but it has physical and mental components as well. Sometimes you may not even realize that you are suffering from test anxiety until you notice the physical symptoms. These can include trembling hands, rapid heartbeat, sweating, nausea, and tense muscles. Extreme anxiety may lead to fainting or vomiting. Obviously, any of these symptoms can have a negative impact on testing. It is important to recognize them as soon as they begin to occur so that you can address the problem before it damages your performance.

The mental components of test anxiety include trouble focusing and inability to remember learned information. During a test, your mind is on high alert, which can help you recall information and stay focused for an extended period of time. However, anxiety interferes with your mind's natural processes, causing you to blank out, even on the questions you know well. The strain of testing during anxiety makes it difficult to stay focused, especially on a test that may take several hours. Extreme anxiety can take a huge mental toll, making it difficult not only to recall test information but even to understand the test questions or pull your thoughts together.

Effects of Test Anxiety

Test anxiety is like a disease—if left untreated, it will get progressively worse. Anxiety leads to poor performance, and this reinforces the feelings of fear and failure, which in turn lead to poor performances on subsequent tests. It can grow from a mild nervousness to a crippling condition. If allowed to progress, test anxiety can have a big impact on your schooling, and consequently on your future.

Test anxiety can spread to other parts of your life. Anxiety on tests can become anxiety in any stressful situation, and blanking on a test can turn into panicking in a job situation. But fortunately, you don't have to let anxiety rule your testing and determine your grades. There are a number of relatively simple steps you can take to move past anxiety and function normally on a test and in the rest of life.

Physical Steps for Beating Test Anxiety

While test anxiety is a serious problem, the good news is that it can be overcome. It doesn't have to control your ability to think and remember information. While it may take time, you can begin taking steps today to beat anxiety.

Just as your first hint that you may be struggling with anxiety comes from the physical symptoms, the first step to treating it is also physical. Rest is crucial for having a clear, strong mind. If you are tired, it is much easier to give in to anxiety. But if you establish good sleep habits, your body and mind will be ready to perform optimally, without the strain of exhaustion. Additionally, sleeping well helps you to retain information better, so you're more likely to recall the answers when you see the test questions.

Getting good sleep means more than going to bed on time. It's important to allow your brain time to relax. Take study breaks from time to time so it doesn't get overworked, and don't study right before bed. Take time to rest your mind before trying to rest your body, or you may find it difficult to fall asleep.

Along with sleep, other aspects of physical health are important in preparing for a test. Good nutrition is vital for good brain function. Sugary foods and drinks may give a burst of energy but this burst is followed by a crash, both physically and emotionally. Instead, fuel your body with protein and vitamin-rich foods.

Also, drink plenty of water. Dehydration can lead to headaches and exhaustion, especially if your brain is already under stress from the rigors of the test. Particularly if your test is a long one, drink water during the breaks. And if possible, take an energy-boosting snack to eat between sections.

Along with sleep and diet, a third important part of physical health is exercise. Maintaining a steady workout schedule is helpful, but even taking 5-minute study breaks to walk can help get your blood pumping faster and clear your head. Exercise also releases endorphins, which contribute to a positive feeling and can help combat test anxiety.

When you nurture your physical health, you are also contributing to your mental health. If your body is healthy, your mind is much more likely to be healthy as well. So take time to rest, nourish your body with healthy food and water, and get moving as much as possible. Taking these physical steps will make you stronger and more able to take the mental steps necessary to overcome test anxiety.

Mental Steps for Beating Test Anxiety

Working on the mental side of test anxiety can be more challenging, but as with the physical side, there are clear steps you can take to overcome it. As mentioned earlier, test anxiety often stems from lack of preparation, so the obvious solution is to prepare for the test. Effective studying may be the most important weapon you have for beating test anxiety, but you can and should employ several other mental tools to combat fear.

First, boost your confidence by reminding yourself of past success—tests or projects that you aced. If you're putting as much effort into preparing for this test as you did for those, there's no reason you should expect to fail here. Work hard to prepare; then trust your preparation.

Second, surround yourself with encouraging people. It can be helpful to find a study group, but be sure that the people you're around will encourage a positive attitude. If you spend time with others who are anxious or cynical, this will only contribute to your own anxiety. Look for others who are motivated to study hard from a desire to succeed, not from a fear of failure.

Third, reward yourself. A test is physically and mentally tiring, even without anxiety, and it can be helpful to have something to look forward to. Plan an activity following the test, regardless of the outcome, such as going to a movie or getting ice cream.

When you are taking the test, if you find yourself beginning to feel anxious, remind yourself that you know the material. Visualize successfully completing the test. Then take a few deep, relaxing breaths and return to it. Work through the questions carefully but with confidence, knowing that you are capable of succeeding.

Developing a healthy mental approach to test taking will also aid in other areas of life. Test anxiety affects more than just the actual test—it can be damaging to your